BAD BOYS
BEHIND BARS

BAD BOYS BEHIND BARS

An Anthology of Prisoners' Narratives

BINANDA C. BARKAKATY

To order additional copies of this book, contact:
Xlibris LLC
0-800-056-3182
www.xlibrispublishing.co.uk
Orders@xlibrispublishing.co.uk
307030

Look among the nations, and see;

wonder and be astounded.

For I am doing a work in your days,

that you would not believe if told.

Habakkuk 1:5, ESV

ACKNOWLEDGEMENTS

- I owe a sense of gratitude to the governor who gave me permission to carry out the mini research, including access to some confidential files for exploring criminogenic attributes of prolific offenders.

- Without the tremendous cooperation of the prisoners, this book would not have come to the public domain. I am truly indebted to them.

- I owe a great deal to my wife, Puspa, for her encouragement and patience during the preparation of *Bad Boys Behind Bars*.

- Last but not least, I would like to remember the unknown person at Kwik Fit South Croydon, who triggered the first inspiration to write about my experience of working in a prison environment and the enigmatic stories hidden behind prisoners' criminal lifestyles.

PROLOGUE

An autumn morning dawned at Sanderstead. The sun was just peeping through the beeches spreading the bright electromagnetic spray to wave welcome to everyone. I had just driven into the local Kwik Fit to see to a small problem in my car causing some concern for a few days. A fine young man wearing a sparkling smile booked my car in and told me that it might take about half an hour.

A tall, smart, well-built middle-aged gentleman had just been talking to a few ladies who happened to be there for their car repairs, laughing and joking. In that reception room, everyone could notice that the gentleman was at the centre stage of conversation. Time was passing by; a few cars had been seen to, and some of the customers, including the smart ladies, had left. I sat down to read the adverts in a glossy car mag. There was only a small round table in front of me, one metre in diameter. I quietly calculated the perimeter as 100π cm for no apparent reasons, still browsing through the pages of the mag. I suddenly realised the approach of a tall shadowy figure towards me, and he put his weight on the chair diagonally opposite me. It was the verbose tall gentleman, who was eagerly looking for someone to begin a conversation with.

First we talked about cars and the associated problems. Then we moved on to how many cars we had been driving over the years, which car was the best, which was the worst, and which was the best value for money. His knowledge of cars far exceeded the knowledge I had accumulated so far. No wonder he was so pleased to share his knowledge with me, sitting opposite me at the small round table. Then, in the middle of our conversation, he asked me about my career, what I had been doing, and where I worked. He seemed very interested and fascinated to hear that I spent seven years working as a manager in a prison education setting. Remarkably, he was exhilarated with some comments made by the inmates and their lifestyles behind bars that I explained to him. His car was ready for collection, the young man at the reception just reported. Standing up, he said, 'You know what? I would like you to write a book on your experience of working with prisoners. I am sure you will be able to throw some light about our misconceptions about our prisons and prisoners. Thank you very much for talking with me. It's been wonderful to chat with you. Goodbye and God bless.' So he left with a big beaming smile.

As I am writing this book, his smile has shone on each section of the book, inspired, encouraged, and blessed. I do not know his name, neither do I know his address. I only wish and pray that the book will reach him one day in not too distant a future to remind him of the conversation we had at Kwik Fit South Croydon which has resulted in the production of this book.

I also owe a great deal to the prisoner clients who are the major players in this anthology for enabling me to expose their side of the story to the general public, the criminal justice system, the policy makers, social services, prison, and the probation services. Their pent-up feelings, anguish, and open voices would have never reached the general public without the publication of this book. I honestly hope this book will provide a fresh insight to the readers about prisoners' life, their lifestyles, and their criminal career, together with the systems that are in place to provide safer custody and promote personal development and employment opportunity for the prisoners towards reducing reoffending.

BAD BOYS BEHIND BARS

Remember those in prison as if you were their fellow-prisoners, and those who are ill-treated as if you yourselves were suffering.

Hebrews 13:3, NIV

The most powerful evangelist, the apostle Paul, knew about the conditions under which the prisoners of the Bible time had to serve their sentences, because he was a prisoner himself. He knew what it was like to be persecuted and to endure sufferings. Paul was a persecutor of the highest degree before he came to be the follower of Jesus Christ. Therefore, he had the knowledge of a persecutor and as a persecuted bearing all trials and tribulations for the sake of the truth which brings salvation to all human beings.

I have started with the quote from the Bible which spells out clearly how we should feel for and treat the ever-increasing number of prisoners in our country today. I am about to unfold the pent-up feelings, burnt-out emotions, and mountains of anguish of some inmates in a high-security prison in England. If everyone working in the prison and probation services were like Paul, who would do all in his power prayerfully to bring fallen, despised, and suffering people to normative human fold, then we may be able to see a streak of sunshine at the end of the tunnel for reducing reoffending.

Let me introduce some of my clients. Don't worry, they are people just like you and me. Just sit down and relax and try to feel the world they live in and that from which they came. They are behind bars, away—far, far away—from their loved ones because they broke the law. We call them prisoners, inmates, incarcerated, and the castaways. We call the place they live in Her Majesty's Prison, and the prisoners call it Her Majesty's Hotel. Yes, for some poor guys the penitentiary could be a haven where they can cast away their day-to-day problems and tuck into a three-meals-a-day service. For the majority, however, it is a place where they are doing their time, having lost their liberty, self-esteem, and personal dignity. The criminal justice system (CJS) has found them guilty of the crimes they have committed.

As you can see, that does not make them inhuman, or does it? They are a small 'community of captives' cast away from a larger community of all other human beings. We are a social creature, law abiding, rule conforming, perpetuating a social structure which we all believe will always follow the norm. One millimetre off the norm-line and we can no longer call ourselves normal. So we can very easily fall into the group of people with antisocial behaviour, especially if you are young, or into the group which has the intentions to carry out criminal offences whatever might be the outcome. The standard of what we call norm is very fine, and it depends on the view of the person who is making the judgement. A crime is a crime defined by law. Activities carried out by deviant motivation are crimes. The criminal offenders are still a part of our society. They fell short of the standard set by the CJS of our country.

CRIMINAL ENTERPRISE AND INQUIRING MIND JUXTAPOSED

At first, meet my very clever and vivacious friend Amos. He is a technocrat and an intelligent person with some sound scientific knowledge. He is presently starting a life sentence for a crime he says he never committed. Don't take his word for it because all prisoners do not believe that they have committed any crime. Isn't it interesting and surprising? It has been shown in research that, especially for the sexual offenders, they would never confess that they have committed any crime; neither would they show any remorse. Anyway, read on what Amos has to say in his open letter to me. Although I have corrected some of his spellings, I have left the grammatical errors for you to grasp his ideas as they appear in the letter. I do not know what motivated him to write this document for me, and I don't claim that I had any influence in making him embark on producing this document. But one thing is sure, Amos is a thinker, and his scientific thinking makes him stretch his mind to enter into many a field which we may not even imagine about. Below is his document handed over to me while we were in prison! You will soon be able to see that prisoners are capable of thinking divergently as any other entrepreneurs.

> We will put to prisons, hospitals, schools, churches, leisure centres, parliament buildings, Buckingham Palace and many more buildings'

roofs solar panels and wind turbines. Also we will do the same for council blocks and private houses. We will take small amount deposit and we will take every month bill payment but we will put interest. When all payments paid we will stop to take monthly bill payment.

A few German solar and wind energy system producers said we want to give to you UK's distributors and we will send to you our products which of those you will need. But you will not pay any money unless you started to earn. When you started to earn and you will start to us with monthly payments without interest.

Railway systems:

1. Digger machines will dig pits (wells) for bedding.
2. Frame worker teams will be fitting structural frames.
3. Electricians will be fitting solar and wind systems. Teams will work three shifts a day seven days a week but labourers will take off two days a week. One team will take off first week, second team second week. We must finish fifty miles per month.
4. Ten digger machines will work (minimum).
5. Ten frame worker teams will work for fitting. Each team minimum ten labourers (minimum ten teams). Each team ten labourers, ten teams hundred labourers.
6. Ten electrician teams will be fitting energy systems. Each team minimum ten technician (minimum ten teams).

That's to say we will give job to minimum two hundred and fifty people including engineers. If we will finish fifty miles a month and if UK's railways length two thousand and five hundred miles we will complete the job in fifty months = 4 years and 2 months. But our life is full of surprises. For this reason we have to think to complete in five years' time. If we need more labourers we will get more, how many is necessary.

We will need minimum another ten electrician teams, each team with ten technicians for prisons, hospitals, schools, churches, leisure centres, town halls, council blocks, private houses, Buckingham Palace and other buildings.

We will work in two different ways:

1. If they do not want to buy the systems, we will get monthly payment but 50% cheaper than UK's electricity energy prices.
2. For example, a council block has 50 flats. System's cost is minimum £25,000. And each flat pays £200 bill a month for summer and £300 for winter. We will charge for six months £100 for 3 months and for other six months £150 for 3 months. That is to say each flat will pay £500 for each year. 50 flats × £500 = £25,000 income each year. System will pay itself in one year. Other year's income will come clean.
3. If they want to buy we will get 25% deposit and after they will pay monthly bill. But we will put interest and profit and when they paid everything we will stop getting monthly bill payment.

For railways: Railway systems will be our systems and we will sell electricity to the government and we will get monthly payment lifetime.

If we will finish 50 miles a month minimum we will finish 12.5 miles a week. That is to say every week 12.5 miles will start produce electric energy. When we finish 100 miles, one hundred miles of electric energy income will help us pay for our expenditure. And at the same time we will start to work on magnetic electric dynamos. We can produce electric cars, buses, motors and village electric systems and end cities electric energy systems. At the end of the five years we will be UK's biggest energy producer and seller company. When all projects are complete we will earn minimum 2.5 billion GBP per year. We will pay 500 million pounds as income tax and 500 million pounds as other expenditure. We will make 1.5 billion pounds profit a year. We will pay 750 million pounds to companies who gave us systems and our clear profit will be 750 million pounds per year. If we can produce electric car engines our income will be minimum £2 billion clear per year. If we will jump to overseas countries you can't imagine our clear income.

My imagination shows that at the end of ten years we will be the biggest electric energy producer in the world. This is not a dream. Please think Bill Gates. He became a billionaire in a very short time and now he is the biggest computer program producer in the world.

Don't think about my situation. My sentence expired. If we submit our projects to the officials concerned I will be able to get release straightaway, because we will be able to help solve electric energy issues and we will be able to provide jobs to minimum thousands of people. And we will also pay minimum 500 million pounds income tax every year. We will be able to export electric car engines to overseas countries. That is to say very importantly we will help develop UK's economy.

We will also start a third step to produce desalination systems to sell to waterless countries. But desalination systems work with electric energy. That's to say at the same time we will sell solar and wind electric energy systems together with desalination systems and we will supply and fit those systems. If all these three systems start to work, we will need minimum workforce of 5,000 people who will include engineers, electricians, construction experts, and others. I believe and I can see the future. You believe me UK officials will kiss our feet and they will give us gold medals and Sir status. That's to say 5 years later Mr Binanda Barkakaty will be Sir Binanda Barkakaty and a gold medallist.

We don't need any money for start because German solar panels and wind turbine companies will send their products without any payment. Structural frame companies will give their products without paying a penny. And Bank of England will give the workforce salaries with very low interest. And we will pay back five years later yearly payment. Please you believe me all of these are not dreams if you look seriously and if you concentrate on the proposed projects. Because we are not stupid, on the contrary, we are very clever and very intelligent. Only we have to start straightaway to succeed. I believe we will succeed you believe me. Now Bank of England's interest rate is 0.5% per year. Bank of England gives capital to companies for the production of more wealth for the development of UK's economy.

In another conversation Amos explained to me that the British prison system is a kind of black hole for our economy. He thinks that about 33 per cent of the prisoners are kept in prisons for offences like thefts, mugging, shoplifting, and common assaults at a colossal cost of £34,000 a year for each of them. Out of the present 88,000 prisoners in the UK, about 29,000 could have been given alternative sentences in a productive way. He suggested that these prisoners could be put in rehabilitation centres in small islands around the UK where self-sustaining communities could be developed away from the areas where these inmates come from. The initial cost will be to develop these centres with enough officials to look after their safety and their daily activities. They will be involved in running a farm, cultivating their own fields, growing their own crops, constructing their own buildings, and running their own businesses. In a few years, such communities, if managed well under efficient management, will not only be self-sufficient but also be able to produce enough to contribute to the economy of the country. Government can work on this type of project, which will save almost a billion pound per year from prison expenses.

According to Amos, the government is a failure as regards the programme on reducing reoffending is concerned. He believes that the prison and the probation service have not been able to tackle the rehabilitation of ex-offenders since well-developed systems are not in place with expertise to provide proper accommodation, counselling, education, support, and training to them. Because of the lack of planned programmes for the ex-offenders to rehabilitate into the communities, they get into trouble with the police and begin the cycle of reoffending, contributing to the revolving-door situation.

Furthermore, Amos told me that he knew some families from the European Economic Countries who had been abusing the housing system. He told me they rented out their council houses and lived abroad, thereby making money at the cost of the taxpayers for many years. So the councils have not been able to bring to justice those people who have been fraudulent in paying income tax and are taking advantage of the system to make money at the expense of others. I must say a criminal can spot other criminals very clearly while even the Crown Prosecution Service may miss out miserably. Take for example the Jimmy Savile case. A prolific sex offender and predatory paedophile, as found by the Savile report now, was at large right in the face of the public for six decades. Yet for reasons beyond explanation, he wasn't prosecuted and brought to justice, although many opportunities to prosecute him presented themselves on several occasions.

Well, that is a short account from my first client, Amos, giving a glimpse into his ideas and thought patterns while being an inmate in a medium-sized British prison. If we put his prison life aside and look at him head-on as he speaks, perhaps we can see a person who can think, make rational arguments, propose illuminating ideas, and view the problems of the wider society. He has accepted the verdict of the judge and has taken his sentence one day at a time as they present.

THERE IS NO LIGHT AT THE END OF THE TUNNEL

Meet my next client, who is sitting next to me as he speaks in his seven-by-nine cell. He is Boros, a tall, slim guy with a distinct lump in his bald patch on his head. It is a reminder that he was hit by a bullet as he was involved in gang fight after a bank raid. Both his arms have deep knife wound marks clearly visible. He lost one eye during a shoot-out. Perhaps you are getting a little bit uneasy with my client! Fear not, he is just a man exactly like you and me. He is from the West Indies. In one of his adventure trips he landed in London looking for some opportunities to make money quickly, as is the case with majority of the offenders. That's why he is with me now revealing some parts of his darker and violent past. He has the gift of the gab. He left school at 14 in Jamaica as he didn't do well in any of his subjects because of his association with the wrong type of peers. His parents took drugs and lived almost hand to mouth, not having any permanent jobs. As they could not look after Boros, like other local kids, he spent most of the time outside his home hanging about with other kids of his own age at street corners, in backyards, and in alleyways. Soon he got involved in stealing, mugging, and taking drugs. As you can imagine, his life trajectory went in the wrong direction. The police arrested him a few times for some minor crimes by the age of 16.

'I left my home and went to Miami at 18 and joined a prominent gang. My life begins at night. I go out with guns in my belt and knives in my pockets. We terrorise the streets of Miami at night. It was exciting, thrilling, and at the same time it was frightening. We may lose our lives any moment. But we used to earn two to three thousand dollars a night.

'I left Miami for London looking for further excitement and criminal opportunities. I was leaving near Brockwell Park with a couple of other guys. We were soon involved in raiding post offices and pubs at nights. Within two weeks of my arrival, the police caught me on the act of robbing a post office. My other friends escaped arrest by quickly driving away in our escape van. I'm on remand waiting for my trial in a month's time. I do not know what the future will bring.'

I saw a heaving and grieving Boros. He was at the end of his tethers. As I watched him closely, he was beginning to sweat. He looked at the ceiling rather blankly, perhaps with a heavy heart, most certainly with the feeling of desperation. He was all alone in a prison cell pondering over his future. He knew it well he would have to pay the price for the crime he had committed against the law of the government. He had enjoyed the exciting time of his criminal career at the cost of many a victim, and now it was his time to accept the sentence which the judge would deliver to him at his court hearing in a few weeks' time. Waiting for the court appearance is a very apprehensive time for any inmate. This is the time when they are most vulnerable. Boros was certainly uneasy thinking about his imminent court hearing, not knowing how long he would be put behind bars.

A HANDFUL OF HAZELNUTS

I met Carlos in the prison a few years back. He was a clean-shaven, well-dressed young man in his early thirties. He told me that he came from Columbia to live in Clapham about ten years ago. He met up with some of his old associates who had been continuing with their criminal career and used to live together. The police caught him while he was selling drugs in Clapham back alleyways. Since then, he had been in and out of prison several times. A homeless, abandoned, and forlorn young man from South America, Carlos had been caught up with the lifestyles of London criminals. He had been entangled in the criminal web from which he found it almost impossible to come out.

Today I met him on board bus number 468 to Elephant and Castle. The bus was pretty full. A well-dressed, thin, tall, and smart young man in his early forties jumped on to the bus, left his handbag and umbrella on the luggage space, and headed for a seat. It seemed I knew his face, but I could not recall who he was. After two stops, when the bus became almost empty, he looked at me from his seat and gave a big smile. He came to sit next to me on my right and asked me whether I could recognise him.

'I am Carlos. Remember me a few years back in the prison?' He quickly removed the cigarette tucked behind his left ear into the left ear. I want to point out to you that in some parts of the world, including my birth place Assam in India, nobody smokes in front of their parents, elders or in front of their teachers. This is to show their respect to and honour their parents, elders, their teachers, and other professionals.

'I have been in and out of prison for the last twelve years. Drug addiction and drug dealing was my career. Every time I have been released from prison, they put me in hostels where I meet my familiar criminal mates and I continue with my criminal career. I'm now very determined not to mix with my old mates and am focussing on building my own future. I requested my caseworker to move me to a faraway hostel to avoid meeting my gang-mates. She agreed to my request, and I'm very happy with my new accommodation.

'I couldn't thank you enough for helping me so much while I was in prison. You have been so kind. I also thank your co-workers who helped us in our personal development. Now I am studying at a local college, doing a course on crane operations. My mind is firmly set on doing a degree course, which my tutors say I should be able to pursue later.'

Putting his hand into his trousers' pocket, he took out a packet of hazelnut and said, 'I don't have anything to give you. But please have some of these, they are really good. Thank you for your kindness and listening to me. I'm now looking upwards, not downwards. I know I have a God-given talent which nobody can take away. It's me who should use it to have a brighter future for me.'

So a handful of hazelnuts did bring a long-time criminal closer to me to open his heart, providing me a glimpse into the practical pathways to reducing reoffending. We both got off at the same stop and bid goodbyes. What a remarkable encounter! What a pleasure sitting next to an ex-convicted criminal who is under conviction of his own conscience now! What a wonderful feeling to know that Carlos has accepted desistance as his pathway to rehabilitation after more than a decade of his life spent as a career criminal.

REMORSE CAME TOO LATE

Here was Dobos in his cell talking to me about his family in Florida. Don't ask me how he arrived in London, but needless to say, he was now an inmate in this prison. He was showing me a letter with some pictures of his family. The letter was sent by him to his parents in Florida several weeks back. Unfortunately, the letter was returned to him exactly as it was. He wrote the letter to inform his mum and dad that he was in custody in this prison and after his trial he might be deported or be kept in prison in England. He was sorry that he made it a mess in coming to England. His father wrote a short note saying that he did not want to know him any more as Dobos had been convicted as a criminal now and his father wouldn't like to be in touch. He stressed that Dobos must not write to them in the future. Dobos then handed me another letter written by his wife where it was clear that his dad wanted his wife and only child of two years out of their house. His lips quivered, his words he swallowed, his head slowly went down to reach the shiny desk. A moment of silence elapsed. He put his head up, heaved a heavy sigh, gathered his strength, and began to speak.

'You know, Binanda, all the past ten years I kept me, mum and dad, and my family happy with the excellent money I had been earning with my crooked ways. I'm violent and cruel when it comes to extracting money from the wealthy people. I have been sending money to my parents to build our parental home and an extension for my own family to live. So long as I sent money to my dad, he was happy knowing perfectly well that I am in no legal business. Neither have I got the qualifications to get a decent job. Now I'm in prison.' He chuckled. 'My dad don't want to know me no more. It's a cruel world. I'm hurting. My dad wants to throw my wife and child from the house built and run by my earnings so far. Where can I go? Who can I go for comfort and any loving word? Although I knew that I would get caught by the police one unfortunate day, I took the gamble of living an exciting life, getting involved in criminal activities. It was my choice. That was my business—criminal business full of surprises, excitement, and high drama, full of high risks. My wife and child are now facing eviction. Soon they will be homeless. It's bloody *cruel*. I'm in a real mess. You know, I feel like committing suicide.'

How does Dobos fare with you? Has he shown any remorse or humanity? Are you compassionate about his young family? Are you angry and upset for the way his dad is treating his own son? Are you hurting as Dobos is in his present predicament? The difference between you and him, however, is significant. You are outside the prison walls enjoying the fresh air with your family and friends. Dobos is behind bars, stripped of his liberty, freedom, self-esteem, and self-confidence for his criminal act in a moment of frenzy. It is a catastrophic moment in which his criminal career suddenly came to an abrupt end, bringing his illusive world of richness, excitement, and fantasy crumbling down.

I don't know what happened to Dobos after I had the meeting with him in his cell. Perhaps he had been transferred to another prison or he had been deported to Florida. Here was a man who had openly confessed that he was an offender by his own choice. He had designed and developed his criminal career. I was not told why he had to resort to criminal activities, nor did he tell me about his family background. It could, however, be easily surmised that Dobos did not have any acceptable level of educational background which could have paved the path for a decent, proper job for him to support his family under normal circumstances. First-time custody in prison prompted him to write to his dad immediately for a word of comfort, love, affection, and encouragement to survive each day in a prison environment. What did he get in return? A complete rebuff from his dad had sent him to the point of contemplating committing suicide.

You might be wondering whether it is possible to commit suicide in a prison cell. It is very common in every prison. Suicide prevention is a big area of service in which vulnerable inmates are carefully monitored 24/7 in their cell by experienced prison officers. In spite of stringent vigilance, prisoners take their own lives in unsuspected circumstances. The governor is accountable if any inmate loses his life while in custody, as prison is a place where the inmates' health, safety, and well-being come first.

HOPE AGAINST HOPE IS NO HOPE

I recall Erol, who was on Rule 45, which means he was regarded as a vulnerable prisoner. It means he might be harmed by other inmates if they came to know his offence. He was in a single cell, and his door was always locked. He always talked to me through the door. Most of the time, I found him sleeping motionlessly in his bed, except at mealtimes when he was allowed to collect his food. I knew him for about six months while he was still on remand waiting for his trial. When the trial was over, he got a life sentence for his violent criminal act of abducting schoolchildren and abusing them for several years. The detail report was published in national and local papers with his photograph. The following morning the officers found him dead in his cell. Was he remorseful for his dreadful criminal activities? Or was he frightened of spending all his days in solitary confinement? Or could it be that he was ashamed of showing his face to the other inmates who had already come to know of his violent criminal act? Perhaps he was very apprehensive facing another day in this world lest he be harmed by his fellow mates.

Erol never told me anything about his past life, never spoke a word. He never discussed anything with me. I didn't see him talk much with other prison officers either. Erol was an unexplainable character. His criminal offence was out in the open in the public domain. But the real man of flesh and blood, of mind, body, and soul will remain as elusive as ever.

WHY AM I SO LONELY IN THE WHOLE WIDE WORLD?

There was another young man from an Eastern European country in his late twenties. He could not speak English well. He was also a drug dealer and a drug addict. He had already been convicted of his crime and was facing a twelve-year sentence behind bars. Some drug addicts are given prescribed dose of methadone to deal with their withdrawal syndrome. Many a time they become very ill, depressed, and withdrawn. They are then transferred to the medical ward where they could be looked after and monitored by the medical staff and nurses. The medical ward is the most depressing and unpleasant ward of all the wards in the whole prison. Most of the inmates in the ward have mental health issues, and the officers have to deal with some difficult and violent inmates.

This young man called Filos was transferred to the medical ward a few days earlier. When he talked to me through the door, he seemed to be quite sober.

'Hello, Filos, how are you doing today?' I smiled at Filos.

'Not good. I feel not good. I remember my mum and dad and also my grandma. Don't know what I do here. I shouldn't be here, you see. I should go outside prison. You good, see me. Prison officers no good. They give medicine and close doors. I sleep and sleep. I think my mum and dad. No family. They don't care. Life no good. No talk to my family.' He then stopped abruptly. I could see streaks of tears rolling down his rosy cheeks over the unshaven beard.

'I hope you will feel better soon. This is the work that you have to complete for this week. See you next week sometime. Goodbye.' I then left with a heavy heart, with Filos's health situation hanging in my mind like a chesty cough.

Two days later after my visit, Filos took his own life in his cell. Whatever background he came from, all we knew was he got caught up in the world of drug dealing and drug taking at an early age. Since he had got a long sentence, he might have been depressed, disoriented, and demoralised under his own conviction. He could have served his sentence and could have come out in his late thirties and be with his family and friends, perhaps living a normal life in the community. Contrary to our views, Filos decided to take his own life at such a young age, leaving all the members of his family to grieve on his departure from this world. I wish I could read his mind to find out why he decided to commit suicide. I wish I could have been of any help, which could have prevented him from his tragic action. One thing is clear, however: he preferred to say a final goodbye to this world to living within the prison walls, under the prison regime, suffering with his health conditions and the pains of bearing the shame for his criminal activities for all his life.

You see, prisoners are human beings, with flesh and blood, and they have sensitivities, emotions, and consciousness even while they are serving their time in prison. A prison is a closed community, essentially cut off from the outside world. Without taking official permission and security clearance, they cannot have any social visits. To make a telephone call, inmates have to get the telephone numbers cleared, get the specific time arranged, and be supervised. It takes almost a week to arrange one telephone call. The inmates become very anxious when they do not hear any news from their loved ones. Not only have the inmates lost their freedom of movement, but they are also required to conform to the prison regime. Some inmates take a longer time to get used to the prison regime, and some try to revolt against some prison conditions. However, all prisoners have the legitimate right to complain about any situations, conditions, or inappropriate behaviours from the prison officers directly to the governor.

Don't you think the prison inmates are a kind of wasted, neglected, and oppressed human community? Contrary to popular belief that prisons are like four-star hotels, I have met no inmate who told me that they liked prison life and would like to carry on with their criminal career, if there is any way that would help them live a so-called normal life. In a recent television interview by Sir Trevor McDonald in high-security Indiana State Prison, one prisoner on a life sentence in a segregation unit commented that if an animal was put in that nine-by-seven cell twenty-four hours a day, seven days a week, it would be frustrated and go crazy within days. Then how much more torture could a human endure living in that situation? That young man who committed double homicide at the age of 13 for just $5 has already served twenty-seven years in high-security prison. He has no experience of a normal adult life. He has not gone to college, driven a car, paid any bills, has any girlfriend or any social interaction for that matter. The prison is his life, and his life is his prison. Yet Sir Trevor finds in his bookshelf books on eugenics and philosophy! The young man wrote in his cell wall:

> No man is an enemy,
> No man is a friend,
> Every man is a teacher.

Once, former Labour Party Home Secretary Jack Straw announced that prisons are meant for punishment and rehabilitation. Looking at the state of our prison and probation systems, it is apparent that while the punishment is guaranteed, rehabilitation of the ex-offenders into the community is far from satisfactory. When an offender is released, at the prison gate he is given about £100 for his survival, and let him walk away. One can easily surmise that this is not in his favour of starting a new life in the community. It is as if to say, 'We have washed our hands of you. It is your responsibility to sort out your mess for which only you are responsible.' Immediately, without anywhere to go, the ex-offender goes to find his comfort zone—the hostel he used to live before where all his old pals live. He is in the criminal web again without any way out for him to change his habit or to find a proper job to build his life. This is where the prison and the probation systems are failing over and again.

A new day in the prison starts with the same regime. Clanging of huge steel doors, shouting of the prison officers calling the inmates for their different activities from education to social visits, movements of the inmates for their destinations set the scene. Simultaneously positioning of the prison officers in their vantage positions, introduction of the new prisoners to the induction unit, movement of tutors, doctors, nurses, chaplains, social workers, and all other trainers, take place like clockwork. All these happen in about forty-five minutes, which is called the free-flow when all the routes to various activity areas are left open for the movement of the prisoners. Even with the keenest of interest and a near-perfect preparation for the free-flow, a few prisoners end up in the wrong places. Once the free-flow is over, inmates settle down in their activities, a routine headcount is done immediately. If the total number of prisoners does not tally with the actual population, a recount is ordered immediately. Occasionally, even with a recount, the headcount does not give the actual prison population, then all prisoners are called back to their cells until the governor is satisfied that every inmate is accounted for.

WHO'S GONNA FEED MY FAMILY?

Are you now ready to meet my next client? I hope you are. He is Giros, a man of 35, with his wife and two children at home. Just after the free flow was over, he came close to me.

'I will be released tomorrow. It's bad time I was out. I have served two years in this shit of a prison. I'm looking forward to seeing my wife and children.'

'I'm very happy for you, Giros. It has been a pleasure meeting you. But one thing I would like to say, I wouldn't like to see you in this prison again. Can you promise that?' I replied.

'Are you kidding? Who's gonna look after my family? Who's gonna feed my baby? I don't have no job to go to. And you know it jolly well how difficult it is for ex-offenders to get employment. So, I must find some means of getting some money to help my family survive. I'm sorry. I must support my family. No one else will do that for me. The government does not want to know our situations. Social services do not care. You know what I mean.'

Giros's answer is saturated with the very ingredients for recidivism that make a perfect offender to continue reoffending without even thinking about the consequences. They wrestle hard with their conscience, but it seems the question of daily survival and maintaining a lifestyle overrides any rational solution. Furthermore, once you are convicted of an offence, you are on the police spotlight. For a repeat offender, it is impossible to avoid arrest for any crime whatsoever.

Employment of ex-offenders is almost impossible because of their criminal record. I had the opportunity to employ some young people under the government's Future Job Funding Project in 2010. Every young person we can employ in our establishment, we get £2,000 if we can keep the employee for a minimum of six months. I created five new jobs within the establishment with job descriptions, person specifications, and contracts. Liaising with the job centre, I was successful in filling three posts and interviewed two young men for the other two jobs. Both of them were very suitable for the posts. In the interview both of them mentioned about their past police arrest and criminal conviction—one for shoplifting and the other for possession of drugs. When I had to process their Criminal Record Bureau (CRB) applications, I encountered insurmountable difficulties. The police investigation section of the CRB could not give clearance and left the decision to be made by us. I could not employ because of the company policy which states that no employment can be provided without a satisfactory CRB check. Those two posts were never filled. I kept the posts for them for about three months, keeping in touch with them regularly. They could not get the jobs just because they had previous criminal records for minor crimes when they were in their teens. How are we then going to help integrate even the minor ex-offenders into the community? The attitude of the society in general and the prospective employers in particular towards employing ex-offenders and helping them in the transformative integration process must change if we are to move forward in the ex-offender employment programme.

EGO, IGNORANCE, AND SELFISHNESS LEAD TO DEVIANCE

Are you getting a little bit worn out, or do you still have some enthusiasm with which you started to hear the stories of my clients from Eric Sykes's community of captives?

Next in the report is Holos, a London-born man who travelled the world from Russia to Brazil as a hard-core gang leader. Don't ask me how he did it, but that's what he told me as he came forward to talk to me about his life.

'I am a Londoner born as a Londoner and perhaps would die as a Londoner. I left school at 16 and followed a criminal career since. I travelled the world from Russia to Argentina, moving from one country to another. Wherever I went I joined the local criminal gang, terrorised the cities with guns and knives, robbed banks and post offices, and made friendship with local women wherever I happened to be. I have to tell you, mate, I love women, and women used to fall for me for some reasons. You can say I'm a womaniser. I even had an Indian woman partner, and we had two kids. I have children all over the places where I have been. I'm a good man—I still send money to my children and partners for their maintenance all over the world.

'All my life I have lived a criminal life, being always involved in different gangs. Life for me is exciting as a gang member, full of adrenaline and oestrogen overflow. There was never a dull moment. I was rich beyond measure then. Mind you, it is a risky life. We manage to dodge the police most of the time. Occasionally, we are arrested and sent to jail for one or two years. It did not bother me much. But once I am out on the street, the police are always at our back like hungry wolves. Bloody bastards, I hate them.'

'How did you get arrested this time? How many years are you going to serve here?' I asked.

'Well, it is a long story. I have to cut it short. When I was the gang leader in Bronx, New York City, things went wrong. Have a look at this tattoo. This is the symbol of the leader of my gang. And I'm really proud of it.'

He rolled his vest up and showed me the big tattoo on his abdomen covering almost down to his groin.

'On a particular night we decided to rob a bank, which went miserably wrong. There was a shoot-out between us and another rival gang. In the shoot-out, I shot a geezer of the rival gang dead. Police chase followed immediately, and arrested me on the same night. I was put in custody in a federal jail. In my trial, I was found guilty of first-degree homicide and sentenced to life imprisonment. For a moment I thought that was the end of my violent criminal career. However, on my appeal, my life sentence was dropped, and they deported me to the UK with the attached condition that I must not return to the United States again.

'That's how I arrived back in London and was arrested by the police on my arrival for some of my pending crimes committed in England. I'm now serving five years. On my release, I'll be allowed to have movement only in a restricted area of a circle with a radius of one mile. My movement will be constantly monitored. I do not regret what I did in the past because I simply do not like to be under the law designed by someone else to suppress your freedom. Do you know, those who make the law and the police are corrupt to the core themselves. But they are somehow not caught and not criminalised, and they look for people like us to target and punish as criminals. I know I am no angel. But I loot, rob, mug, and raid for my survival and for those I have to feed. That said, I wouldn't like to advise anybody to follow my career.

'I am now 45. It's time I gave up my criminal career. But I haven't prepared anything for my retirement yet.'

Even when he was talking to me, unlike some other offenders that I know, Holos did not show any remorse for his violent actions and criminal past. He was proud to be a gang leader leading an exciting life, he told me. His criminal career was his own choice, not forced upon by a third party. It is apparent Holos did not make any attempt to conform to the structure and law of a so-called normal society. His life was littered with notoriety of the highest level, devoid of any moral conscience, and flavoured heavily with the elements of excessive narcissism.

In front of me there is a man sitting like a mountain which cannot be moved even by the greatest seismic waves. He is engrossed in his own ideology, ego, and anarchistic views. Except his own world, the outside world does not seem to mean anything to him. He finds self-fulfilment in all his deviant thoughts, violent activities, criminal enterprises, and achievement in earning a living even by taking human life. It transpires that his human instincts, emotions, love, and affection are frozen to absolute zero when it comes to achieving his personal goal by unlawful means. His enduring pride takes over whenever he wants to talk about his life. There is no mention of his parents and families. He doesn't blame anyone for his life, though. But one thing is apparent, that he does not like the upper crust of our society, the law makers, the police, and the criminal justice system. He does not like to be bound by societal rules and regulations. You could almost feel his struggle to free himself from the bondage of socially constructed policies, laws, and rules, which are a requirement to conform to the society. His aspirations are much higher than the available means with which to achieve them. This ultimately results in his deviant actions, indomitable drive, uncompromising attitude, and insatiable desire to terrorise victims and to conquer the world.

How are you doing with Holos? Do you think he is a typical prisoner? He is surely a typical ex-offender who would go through the revolving door time and again, and seemingly, there is no pathway for him to change his criminal lifestyle to adopt a transformative rehabilitation. If you strip him of his colourful criminal robe, you will still find a human being with a mind and a world of his own. He is made up of the similar DNA, amino acids, molecules, atoms, protons, electrons, neutrons, and quarks like all of us. Yet he has a mind-set, attitude, and attributes that are diagonally opposite to those of normal human beings. He will be leaving the prison setting in a few years' time. Have we got the appropriate assessment tools available to carry out the risk—assessment for him? Are correctional strategies in place to rehabilitate a hard-grafted criminal like Holos? Should we be at all concerned with a person who has spent almost half his entire life in crime? I think we should. If we are successful in providing a pathway for Holos to reintegrate into the society, then we will know that our system is based on human rights and on transforming ex-offenders to build self-confidence to lead a normal life once again. Reducing reoffending, educating ex-offenders, and empowering them with enterprising skills should be a way forward for the prison and the probation services. In my assumption, we are still far behind in terms of correctional procedures and services to the ex-offenders compared with those available in the United States and in Australia.

CAN A CONVICTED CRIMINAL BE A CHANGE AGENT?

Whatever your views about Holos, I hope you are ready to meet my next client. He is Ipos, another Londoner who has been serving four years of his eight-year prison term for his violent temper, which resulted in grievous bodily harm (GBH). He knew that he has got the punishment that he deserved by law for his serious crime. So he took prison life as a place to make a positive change for himself, and perhaps he would be an example who could change other young offenders. He took prisoner learning journey seriously and took part in important correctional interventions attending courses in education, drug awareness, personal development, and information technology. He also became a listener with training facilities provided by the Samaritans. Soon Ipos made some impact on the prison officers, education tutors, prison chaplains, and the governor, who was a forward-looking and positive activist in looking at the whole issue of the complexity of reducing reoffending.

Ipos told me he had eight children and several grandchildren. He admitted his childhood was smeared with violent activities, street fighting, stealing, mugging, and drug taking, which continued till he was in his late twenties. His violent temper accentuated with his addiction to drugs had a catastrophic effect on his family. He is now 45, a man with a violent past, learning to unlearn his past habits, missing his family badly, and desperately learning new skills and technology to become a changed man when he is released. He believes it is not too late to change for the better. He took an externally examined course on introduction to counselling provided by the National Extension College and was successful. He has embarked on a first-year sociology course with the Open University. He has just completed the programme Family Man, which has opened his eyes about how to build broken family relationships. He has been acting as a listener to provide support and guidance 24/7 to the inmates who are in desperate need to talk to someone about their concerns. Ipos has been actively engaged in special meetings of the correctional teams with the local business communities. He told he would like to commit himself to the community work with the local community for providing information, advice, and guidance to the local vulnerable young men.

He admits openly that no inmate would like to live in a prison confined in a 9 × 7 cell with another fellow inmate on a long-time prison sentence. He says he is so fortunate and grateful in that he has been given permission to go out of the prison on day visits to counsel young adults in the community to tell them about the effect of being a prisoner, how it affects self-respect, self-esteem, emotions, and the whole personality. He has also been able to explain to them what the result of taking or dealing with drugs is. Having gone through the criminal cycle himself, Ipos talks candidly about how he feels to live in a prison cell, being stripped of personal freedom and dignity. He also manages to bring young minor offenders and potential serious offenders into the prison with the permission of the governor. These young men are shown in detail the whole procedure when a prisoner is brought into prison—from stripping of the whole body, through the first shower, into the prison clothes, then taking the net bag of personal needs for the first night in the cell. They are shown the nine-by-seven cell, with two inmates locked in, the toilet just at the side of the bed clearly visible; the television is on a small table which also is the place with tea—and coffee-making facilities. They are also taken to the segregation unit where the vulnerable prisoners are given their solitary confinement 24/7 under strict supervision. Therefore, these young potential offenders have a complete overview of the consequences of being in a prison if they commit any criminal offence. This is quite a telltale picture for these young men who have potential criminal minds. They have seen the harsh lifestyle that any inmate has to endure as a captive criminal. It is, therefore, up to them to make a choice whether to follow a criminal pathway or to change their minds to train themselves for employment opportunities to integrate into the society before it is too late.

Ipos is fully committed to desistence, he told me. He acknowledges it would take time to heal the wounds, but he is prepared to give it a priority whatever it takes. He prefers living with his family to living a criminal life. I know Ipos is a tough guy who lived a violent and turbulent life, breaking up his family. He is now experiencing the love and affection of his family and friends who are coming closer to him. He has found the joy of being a father and a granddad is overwhelming, and it takes him back to his roots. He would be out into the community in a few years, and he has made a few inroads into the process of transformative reintegration already. Personally, I believe he has the willpower and the basic foundation to rebuild his life. Who knows, I may bump into him in a bus station, on a train, or even in a busy shopping mall in London one day! Well, let's hope so.

Isn't he an interesting character, my friend? Prison has made him a new person with a new vision of being a change agent for others. Looking at Ipos, it emerges that a prison has a lot to offer in terms of opportunities for a hard-core criminal to change himself. The intervention programme at the prison must therefore be robust, interesting, person oriented, and employment focussed. The programme developers and deliverers must take into account these factors, which will ultimately impact on the inmates to make their minds up about desistance. The responsibility of the programme developers and the deliverers in bringing about lasting changes on prisoners cannot be overestimated. At the end of the day, however, it is the prisoner himself who will have to come forward to accept desistance for a better future for him and his family, as my client Ipos did. The attitude of the prison officers and the governor must have a progressive and positive overtone in order to work together towards reducing reoffending and providing inroads to desistance.

IS MONEY AT THE ROOT OF ALL CRIMINALITY?

Causes of criminality can take many colours—drug, jealousy, ego, fraud, money, honour, and sex. An analysis of the causes of criminality suggests that the top of the list must go to money, which is at the root of majority of the criminal offence. It has also been published that almost 50 per cent of the inmates lack knowledge of basic literacy and numeracy, and almost 67 per cent of the inmates have some sort of mental disorder. That is why while I was interviewed at Cambridge for a postgraduate course, I asked the professor, 'If such an overwhelming proportion of prisoners have mental conditions, why can't we put them all in psychiatric hospitals and do the appropriate treatment for individuals, minimising a colossal amount of prison cost and at the same time making the others well to rehabilitate into the society?' The professor's answer was very clear. 'Yes, you are right in your statement, but it needs refinement. We just cannot put majority of the offenders in one basket labelled mentally imbalanced and wash our hands of them as if they did not commit any crime and so avoid going through the criminal justice procedure. To be honest, some of them in that category have committed atrocious crimes. It is for the reason of equitable justice for all offenders that we cannot put the medical category away without bringing them to justice like the rest of the offenders.

'We all know that it is the deviant mind which helps carry out all crimes. The very word "deviant" albeit might have some medical undertones. That said, an offender with a recognisable mental condition cannot have his offence blotted away just for his mental condition. You see, that's why criminology is such a fascinating and intriguing branch of studies.'

Ah, where am I? I was about to tell you about a young man called Jacob who has got a twelve-year sentence for his involvement in credit card and passport forgery and illegal money laundering. He is a well-educated person of 32 who has been found guilty of the above crimes along with two of his friends who are in other prisons. It is therefore an organised crime. You wouldn't believe what a fine gentleman Jacob is. He is always well dressed, well groomed, and always with a huge smile, which seems innocent enough to make a wrong judgement on him. Like our Ipos, he has adapted to the prison life with a positive mind. After completing his personal development course in the education department, Jacob is concentrating on developing his skills in information and communication technology. He has enrolled himself for the first-level sociology course from the Open University and also on an Understanding the Bible course with the Bible Book Company. I have organised the relevant funding for these courses for him, and he is doing very well in his exams. He is a member of the Education Committee where he makes excellent contributions. He has taken the Bible and the gospels as his main instruments to change him to become a new person.

Having completed the Alpha course at the chaplaincy, Jacob got baptised at the prison chapel. He talked openly and confidently that he needs God's help and forgiveness in order to change his old self. He is now a new creation, Jacob says. When I visit his wing during lunch hour, I could see his cell full of other inmates singing to and praising the Lord. One cannot help thinking why a person can find God inside the prison but not outside! I have to point out at this point that many prisoners seemingly do seek God's help in the prison because of the situation they have found themselves in after committing crimes, living away from their family, friends, and the loved ones.

Jacob is a hard-working young man with a high level of intelligence and kindness to his fellow inmates. He does not talk about his past activities much. Neither does he apparently show any remorse for his crime, as if to picture his crime is not as bad as some other crimes committed by some of his fellow inmates. He is changing in his attitude to and perception of criminal activities. He is also changing inwardly, accepting divine God to change him, depicting his human frailty and vulnerability. He has also shown compassion to his fellow prisoners and would like to see them giving up their criminal career by following his divine pathway, accepting God to intervene, to change their mind-set, views, attitudes, and inner beings. Clearly Jacob has made positive contributions to these prisoners in terms of understanding the importance of desistance as opposed to continuing with their offending behaviour. Jacob has unwittingly made some contribution to the programme of reducing reoffending. As he has got such a long sentence, I wonder whether he would have the strength and willpower to continue his divine campaign until he is released and beyond.

GREED AND ABUSE OF POSITION LEADING TO CRIMINALITY

Keeping on the divine track, I would like you to meet my next client, Kimon. He is 40, with his wife and two teenage boys and a girl of 9. He has been working with the UK Border Agency for the last five years and has gained quite a good deal of knowledge. He was born abroad, studied in London, and got naturalised and finally got his United Kingdom passport. He became a teacher for a while, but got tired of daily heavy and monotonous load of work. Then he tried for a position with the UK Border Agency, and he was offered a post. He was employed at one of the busiest airports in London. Now he is in a shared single cell at this prison. His door was open. I wanted to have a one-to-one conversation with him.

'Hello, Kimon, can I talk to you?' I asked him politely.

'Please do come in,' he replied with a dry smile.

He told me to sit down on a chair while he sat down on his bed. He opened the conversation first as if he expected I was going to ask him about his alleged offence. Kimon said, 'I do not know why I am here. I have not committed any offence, yet they arrested me and put me in custody. I know the Lord will vindicate me. I have been working for years to be a minister in the Church of England. Last year all procedure was complete, and I was due to be ordained in three months' time. Now look, what has happened to me?

Why should a man who loves God end up in prison? Shall we pray to God right now for his intervention in my case?'

He then started to pray for about two minutes. I asked him when his court visit would be and what could he expect. He was full of confidence that the Lord would intervene and vindicate him. The court hearing would be in three months from that day. I wished him good luck and returned with a myriad of questions in my mind without any answers.

Kimon told me he would be interested in doing a course on theology from the Open University if he got a longer sentence. This showed that he might be expecting the worse and he might have been engaged in a criminal activity. He wanted to wait till the court appearance and the verdict. The day of the hearing came, and the jury found him guilty of abuse of his position in a responsible government department. Together with that, Kimon was found guilty of allowing illegal drugs to pass through customs for about three years. Therefore, under the guise of a religious man, Kimon had been heavily engaged in trafficking drugs, taking huge remuneration for his part in it. It became suspicious for his neighbours that within a few years he bought flashy cars and a very expensive house. Someone brought the matter to the attention of the police, and they watched Kimon's activities for many months to be sure to arrest him and finally convicted him of his part in illegal drug trafficking. The severity of the offence lies in the fact that Kimon was a civil servant with vested trust and responsibility to look after the security of the country. Yet the prospect of being rich with illegal drug trafficking completely blinded him from his responsibility. His work with churches and his intention of being a minister seemed to be a ploy under which he could hide his criminal career.

No doubt he is a clever person. Unlike the general trend of criminality, his past life was normal in that he had proper education, including higher studies, he had a normal parental upbringing, and he started his working life with a proper job. From his life profile, there was not a hint of deviance or criminal activity about Kimon until he joined his civil servant position as a customs officer at the airport. So a criminal career can begin at any stage of life, and many a time it seems that a trigger point presents itself to change the course of a normal, stable mind towards criminal pathways. In Kimon's case, it was the intense drive to gain greater financial reward by allowing a huge amount of class A drugs to pass, worth millions of pounds, through customs and taking part in the drug dealing activities himself. Although he knew the severe consequences of illegally smuggling drugs and dealing in drugs in this country, the lure of a large amount of money to be gained so easily obliterated his rational conscience. The temptation of living in a luxurious house, driving flashy cars, and having expensive holidays seemed to override Kimon's conscience. Interestingly, he perhaps forgot to pray or talk to his Lord regarding his act of dealing in drugs. He did not even think about the position he held, which required total professional integrity for the security of the country. He did not do the criminal act just once—it became an addiction. He continued for a few years until he was caught. In fact, the result was a catastrophic life-changing event for Kimon. He turned into a criminal entrepreneur.

As can be expected, Kimon got a heavy sentence of fourteen years and was transferred to another prison. After his trial, the whole story was published in national papers. Nobody could believe that a person who was to be ordained to be a minister in a church could get involved in a drug-dealing circuit. Criminality does not know any boundary. It seems it is like a cancer, can attack anybody, at any age, embracing any profession, any gender, and any colour. As our living conditions and standards are changing, as the technology is developing at an unimaginable rate, people's needs and wants seem to be expanding like a helium balloon. For some people the available means and requirements of securing a job do not match their expectation. They simply follow the easiest of the paths—the criminal highway—to achieve their expectations. In Kimon's case, the usual trajectory of a criminal career did not apply till he saw the criminal route himself in a job which provided the opportunity to embark on an illegal enterprise. It can be easily concluded that it is the love of money and high-flying living that fully engulfed him to commit the offence. I wonder what Kimon is going to do after he spent his time. Certainly his criminal stain will minimise his chances of getting a responsible job. I also think his religious venture is in tatters because he has lost the trust and respect of so many churchgoers. It is conceivable that he would desist and not get involved in criminal activities again because of the severe punishment that the justice system imposed on him. He might also ask God's forgiveness for his action and turn a new leaf for himself and for his family.

Kimon was not a born criminal. He certainly did not have the criminogenic factors which contribute to serious offending. He did not have any peer pressure or any other social interactions which could persuade him to commit crime. Yet he has been incarcerated for an offence for which he alone is responsible. When I met him, he totally denied his involvement with any crime. He tried to show he was a man of God following a right path for living. This goes to demonstrate the frailty and weakness in people that play an important part in criminal activity. It seems everyone is prone and vulnerable to criminality. A crime could be termed minor or major, yet all crimes involve a criminal mind. Given the environment, the condition, and the ingredients, a human mind can easily succumb to illegal activities. These are simple theories but might just fit for some offenders very well. This conclusion is similar to the biblical gospel principle that in God's sight we are all 'sinners' and fall short of the glory of God. Kimon and Jacob are two characters who seem to be diagonally opposite in terms of divine intervention in life. According to Kimon, he followed a religious path and fell from righteousness when he engaged himself in the drug-smuggling activities. Jacob, on the other hand, found God in the prison as a divine helper to turn him around from the criminal path. That said, Kimon's religious past was not the reason for his crime; rather it was his religious living that kept him in the right path until he succumbed to greed, greed, and more greed.

SEX TRADE AT ITS LOWEST

Let's meet my next client, Liam. He is 30 and from an Eastern European country. Liam is a young, strong, and chatty person, always with a big smile. After his arrival at the prison, I went to visit him in his cell as a routine. He has already been convicted of his crime, and he has to spend nine years behind bars. There is diplomatic discussion between the UK and his country about the possibility of his deportation so he can serve his remaining sentence in his own country. He called me into his cell and told me to sit on his bed as there was no chair available at that time. He thanked me for visiting him and sat comfortably on his bed next to me.

'Young man, what brought you here, to this awful place?' I opened the conversation.

'Well, I came to London about four years ago, first just to see the city, second to explore the possibility of a business. I met another three friends from my country who had been living here for several years. We lived together in a rented house in North London. My friends introduced me to their business which had been running well for about two years, they said. They told me that they brought young girls as young as 12 from their own country with the promise that they would provide them with jobs in England. Each girl had to pay £3,000 up front to arrange for their travel and accommodation. Once they got the girls here, they were required to join the sex trade to earn sufficient money each day from the clients to pay my friends and for their accommodation. The thought of earning such a large amount of money every month through the girls, with such an easy way, seemed very compelling and interesting to me. Of course, there was nobody to advise me except my friends as I am so far away from my family. I agreed to be a partner in my friends' business. We continued with our girl trafficking and the sex business without being caught by the police. One of the girls once refused to carry on with the business and requested us to send her back to our country. But we told her that her life would be at risk if she left us.

'One evening she went to the red-light area for usual business and went straight to the police. The police gave her protection and kept her in a safe place. When she did not return to her room, we knew that something wrong had happened. We discussed between us and planned to leave the place to go somewhere else. By the time we were contemplating what to do, the police had already arrived and arrested us and took us to the police station. That was about four months ago. In the trial we were found guilty of trafficking girls illegally and being involved in an unlicensed sex trade using underage girls. I was given nine years, and my friends received twelve years each. I do not know where the other three are, they are in different prisons.

'I'm sorry I got involved in illegal sex business without thinking about the consequences, but I must say I am responsible for what I did. I deserve the sentence I have been given. I have my mum and dad and my girlfriend at home. They know now that I am in prison. I will have to bear this shame for all my life. All I know, I will have to serve my time—that is the reality. I don't think anybody including you will show sympathy for me. I am keeping myself fit by going to the gym regularly and would like to keep my brain ticking if you could organise a course on introduction to bookkeeping for me please.'

I thanked him for opening his heart to me and assured him that I would complete the application procedure for his course in about two weeks' time after he completed the necessary forms. There is another young man caught in the criminal net without even much preparation. We do not know, however, whether he was involved in any criminal enterprise back home. It is very likely that he knew about what his friends were up to in England. He also might have known the high level of risk and possible prison term associated with the sex trade and illegal human trafficking they were running. Their business can be treated as an unacceptable slave trade. They coerced the innocent girls with good jobs and brighter future in the UK. The girls had to live under appalling conditions and had to sell their bodies for sexual pleasures of the punters, earning money for corrupt, incorrigible, and manipulative people like Liam and his friends. They know it very well that what they have been engaged in is illegal and inhuman.

Despite such information available to him prior to his engagement, Liam joined in the criminal act. You may or may not sympathise with him for his long sentence, which he has to serve, but one thing is clear: without any proper job to maintain a lifestyle that a young person wants, without the necessary education and skills to acquire a proper job, Liam found it much easier to jump into the whirlpool of criminal world. This may be due to 'ontogenetic' effect, which relates to the fact that offender behaviour is the result of lack of self-control. This may continue throughout the life cycle of a career criminal. Liam's case might have been the result of 'social interaction' in which he lacked self-control and joined his peers in the illegal act, and they all have to pay the price of their action. I know nobody will sympathise with him. He was involved in an evil, immoral, and inhuman act of human oppression, manipulation, trafficking, and slavery in the twenty-first century. I believe after his release he could still be given appropriate correctional intervention to change his attitude towards crime and provided training and employment skills in order to reintegrate into the society. He could also be trained to impart counselling services to the young offender-in-waiting. Liam completed the course on introduction to bookkeeping while in this prison, and just after that he was transferred to another prison. I wonder whether he was deported to his own country.

HATRED AND VIOLENCE—OFFENDING PARTNERS

Meet my client Milos, a young man of 28 who arrived in the prison five days ago. He is in custody because of his alleged offence of involvement in a house robbery. He is on remand and is waiting for his trial. A prison officer rang me to tell about Milo and requested me to see him. I went to see him just before lunch in his cell and saw a young black man walking one side of the cell to the other. His door was locked. I looked through the peephole. Milos seemed to be restless, deep in his own thoughts, still moving to and fro. He didn't know I was there. I knocked at his door gently. Of course, he didn't know who was coming to see him. Perhaps he got startled. He looked through the peephole and asked me who I was and why I was there to see him.

I explained that an officer telephoned me to have an interview with him to discuss about any course he wanted to do as he seemed to be a very intelligent person. I also told him that while he was on remand I could process the application but couldn't apply for funding from the Prisoners Education Trust. He would have to wait till his court hearing was over. Milos jumped at the idea and proposed that he would like to do a course on

39

business studies, which would help him develop his own small business he had in his mind. He didn't say what the business was. While he was talking to me, I could see he was panicky and restless. He didn't look like a serious candidate for higher studies, although I was informed that he even attended university. I told him that I would go ahead and bring in the application and other forms for him to fill in.

Four days later I went to see him without checking the wing register. To my surprise, he was released only with some conditions attached. I didn't know his history of crime or his family background. I didn't find him an interesting offender to look at his profile until about five weeks later when I saw his picture on television. The police arrested Milos for murdering a lawyer and his wife in cold blood in broad daylight. The report also pointed out that he had previous offences connected with his mental health conditions. The newspaper report detailed that in that fateful morning Milos dressed up as a postman delivering parcels. He appeared in front of the house of the lawyer and knocked at the door. When the gentleman opened the door, Milos took his shotgun out and blasted him with one shot straight through his heart. His dead body lay on the floor, and Milos still stood on the doorstep with his loaded gun. When the wife came out to see what had happened, Milos shot her too, blinded by hatred and violence.

It is a tragic story. Two innocent lives have been taken away by a violent and supposedly mental offender of the highest degree. It is unbelievable that such callous, calculated, and cold-blooded murder could be carried out by a young man whom you have seen in his prison cell about six weeks ago. An offender who showed interest in studying for a university course at one time turned into a well-planned, horrific murderer in broad daylight. Milos's unstable mental condition, coupled with his offending behaviour, made the risk assessment process almost impossible. Undoubtedly, he was found not a risk to the society when he was released from the prison, and he was not monitored carefully about his daily movement. This is where risk assessment tools fail when the offender is associated with multiple-personality disorder or multiple health conditions. On hindsight, everyone can say that it was wrong to release him when the prospect of him reoffending was so great because of his previous reoffending behaviour. On the other hand, if the risk assessment shows that he was not a risk to the general public, the conclusion can be drawn that he shouldn't be kept in prison occupying a prison cell. In this case, surely the assessment went dreadfully wrong, resulting in serious consequences. It is conceivable that the assessment tools like Asset and OASys, widely used in the UK prison and probation services, cannot always accurately predict the future recidivistic behaviour, especially when it is applied to offenders with mental conditions.

Usually the risk assessment analysis is carried out by using the available assessment tools by a prison or probation officer, a psychologist, or a forensic scientist. It is therefore probable that there are apparent problems associated with operationalisation and contradiction in the process between the offender and the interviewing officer. For most offenders with mental disorder, the risk assessment becomes more inaccurate because the answers to the assessment questions from the offender become unacceptable more often than not as the offender struggles to take part in the two-way interactive assessment. Sometimes the assessment cannot be carried out at all because of the prior mental and physical condition of the offender. At other times, the process breaks down halfway through when the offender decides not to proceed any more because he is tired of answering so many questions for so long.

I have given you a snapshot of the assessment processes practised in prison and probation services when a prisoner needs to be released into the outside world. You can see for yourself now how difficult the process of risk assessment could be. Like Milos, there are many such instances where risk deflation resulted in the ex-offender committing horrendous crime. The recent example is of Nicola Edgington, who stabbed her own mother to death for which she was given two years' prison sentence for manslaughter on the grounds of diminished responsibility. When she was released, she went on to stab one woman, and another woman was stabbed to death. Again it had been found that she had mental disorder. The risk assessment conducted after the first stabbing was definitely deflated to allow her to be released, leading to further stabbing. Occasionally, however, risk inflation occurs as a result of assessment. In that case the prisoner has to stay inside the prison for a longer time than he has to.

You must be wondering what this assessment is for. When an offender is incarcerated, he does go through a rigorous assessment procedure in order to explore his criminogenic attributes and other rehabilitation needs. The assessment will flag out his short-term priority needs inside the prison as well as long-term needs for his transformative reintegration programme when he is released from the prison at the end of his sentence. The more accurate and robust the assessment is, the more focussed the intervention programmes will be for the inmate. This in turn helps the ex-offender to be reintegrated safely into the society without putting the public or the ex-offender at risk. Therefore, it is of utmost importance to establish a robust prisoner rehabilitation agenda

41

by the prison and the probation services with a strong focus on reducing re-offending and promoting reintegration. Too many stakeholders in the criminal justice sector also make the whole system vulnerable to rigorous scrutiny. The OASys2 risk assessment tool, used extensively in London prisons, incorporates eleven criminogenic attributes. They are offending information, accommodation, education, training and employment (ETE), financial management and income, relationships, lifestyles and relationships, drug misuse, alcohol misuse, emotional well-being, thinking and behaviour, and attitude. Each element has a different level of score. The maximum total score is 168. The higher the total score is for an offender, the greater is the risk associated with him. However, it is the individual element having the highest score that will highlight his immediate risk needs, which need to be addressed in terms of successful intervention.

Across London prisons, London Initial Screening and Referral (LISAR) scheme, as a general assessment instrument, has been in use for a few years. This assessment is carried out for all inmates on the second day of their reception in the prison. While LISAR does not directly provide the information on the potent factors contributing to recidivism, it highlights the static factors that are dominant attributes of the offender's criminal behaviour. This also acts as a powerful instrument for referring the offender for appropriate help and support to the relevant agency in the prison. Appropriate correctional intervention includes Enhanced Thinking Skills (ETS), Short-Duration Project (SDP) for drug addicts, Anger Management, Prison Addressing Substance-Related Offence (PASRO), Education, Physical Education, and Chaplaincy Services.

The first generation of risk assessment tools are based on clinical assessment and conclusions drawn by professionals. The second generation of tools include Salient Factor Scale, which mainly focuses on static factors of recidivism. The third generation of instruments include Community Risk/Needs Management Scale and Level of Service Inventory-Revised (LSI-R). As I have mentioned earlier, OASys2 has been widely employed as an important tool for predicting recidivism. This also incorporates the Offender Group Recidivism Score (OGRS), which provides the probability of reoffending over a period of twelve months or twenty-four months. Although I haven't elaborated the functionality of these assessment instruments, I thought you would appreciate how many different assessment tools there are. An accurate risk assessment for predicting reoffending behaviour of a prisoner protects the public and the ex-offender and enhances the probability of transformative reintegration.

MENTAL DISORDER—RECIPE FOR CRIMINAL DISASTER

It looks as though you are bored with assessment instruments and strategies for ex-offender rehabilitation. As prison and probation services are established for the purposes of safer custody of prisoner and ultimate rehabilitation, we cannot talk about prisoners without mentioning about rehabilitation. I would like you to meet my next client, Nilor. Born in Belfast, he has been in and out of London prisons and hospitals for the last six years, and he has another four years to serve. He is now 32. And single. He is the first inmate I met in the medical wing which prompted me to develop the agenda for In-Cell Education (ICE) Project. I went to meet him in his cell as advised by the head of education. What I saw was a scene I would never forget. He was in a single cell without any bed, only the four walls and somewhere to sit and write. I went to give him some pencils, colouring pencils, and drawing paper. Both of his arms were in bandages—blood and fluid were oozing out. He slashes his hands with razor blades and any other sharp objects perhaps to show his anger and frustrations of being in a prison. He was not wearing anything when I visited. I came to know that he was arrested on terror charges and he has been in prisons ever since. Nilor told me, 'I should not be in prisons at all, I am innocent. I am not a terrorist. I just speak out my mind. I think about my girlfriend in Belfast and my families. I should be released without any charge. I hate the bloody English, they want to arrest whom they want, they hate us the Irish. Why should they rule us the way they want? They hate us even in the prison. The bloody prison officers don't give me things I want. These bastards think I am mad. I think they are mad to put me in this cell. I thank you for the materials. I'm gonna draw a beautiful picture to send to my girlfriend.'

Suddenly Nilor shouted out, 'Listen to me, you are mad. You are bloody mad. Not me. You are bloody racist. You have no right to hold me in prisons. Do you hear me? You bloody rascals.'

Everybody could hear Nilor shout even from the other end of the wing. Nobody, however, came to see what he was up to.

The next time I went to see Nilor, it was even worse. I couldn't see him. His cell was covered up. Nilor smeared his faeces all over the door—top, sides, and the bottom. All the walls had been smeared with his faeces too. Nasty smell was everywhere. He was inside, no one could see him. All I could hear was shouting inside the cell. I was told he became very aggressive and shouted at everybody. Two prison officers were standing just near the door. They told me that his room had to be washed thoroughly and fumigated.

Before that, he must be moved to a new cell. A couple of days later, he was sent to a psychiatric hospital where he stayed for about three weeks. Then he was back again in the medical wing, and I was able to talk to him again. This time he was well dressed. I could see his slashed arms as he was wearing a short-sleeved shirt. He was calm, quiet, and smiling. He brought a picture of a bouquet of flowers drawn by him. At the top he wrote, 'To my sweetest girlfriend, Mandy.' At the bottom he wrote, 'Yours in love, Nilor.'

'This is what I have drawn for my Mandy. I'm gonna send this to her by post. She will know that I still love her. I'm gonna see her one day. That's my dream. But these bastards are still keeping me in prison shit. They are stupid to bang me up like this. They are racist. They don't like us. I should not be in prison in the first place. Thank you for seeing me, Binanda.'

You see, my friend, how bizarre the prison life could be. Think about the prison officers, doctors, and nurses. They get all the slanders in the world, yet they bear them with a smile. Their work requires that the well-being and safety of the inmates are a priority. A prison is a conjecture, a puzzle, a nightmare. The prisoners are kept behind bars not only for the protection of the public but also for them. One inmate can harm any other prisoner seriously, because of hatred for the crime he committed or because of his mental condition or because of his phobia. They set their own standard as if some crimes can be tolerated but the others cannot. A GBH offender may openly hate a rapist, a serial robber may spit at a paedophile, a double murderer might hate an offender who killed a child. On the other hand, some prisoners get gelled together and become lifelong friends for whatever reasons we would never know. As we have inbuilt inequality in our society, the prisoners create inequality within the inmate community too. As it emerges, the human community cannot just give up class divisions. It is surprising and ironic that we talk about equality in every sphere of our daily life, yet the more we like to embrace the word 'equality', the farther it seems to travel away from you at the speed of light to the dark corner of the horizon.

Nilor cannot just accept his mental disorder, although it is so obvious that he could hardly be away from the psychiatric hospital more than a month. While he would be chatting with me, opening his heart in a soft voice, he would shout with obnoxious words to the prison officers at the top of his voice. I wonder whether he remembers that he was talking to me stark naked the other day. If the justice system found him guilty of taking part in terrorist activities, he says he should not have been put into prison. He is a self-harmer, releasing his anger and frustration by slashing his arms over and over again. As he is a terrorist, his arrest, conviction, and incarceration are justified. He is a prisoner of conscience. But without proper psychiatric treatment, his mental disorder would be worse, and he would have to spend most of his life in prison confinement because he would remain a risk to the society. I believe a prisoner like Nilor would better serve his time in a psychiatric prison, where he would have his required treatment, which might just help him prepare for his release to be integrated into the community. He hates the prison, the prison officers, and above all, the criminal justice system. The system as a whole, to Nilor, is unfair. He is furious within, resulting in his spontaneous outbursts of anger and frustration. However, he is crying out for freedom, love, and community environment, which are simmering in the nook of his heart.

The overcrowding of the prisons causes enormous problems in placing prisoners in the right establishments so they can be provided with suitable intervention programme according to their criminogenic needs. It transpires that when the judges need time to decide about the offenders' sentence, they put them in custody straightaway. So often it is found that some prisoners in custody are not guilty, yet they have been occupying prison cells for months and on. This is unhealthy for the offender and costly for the state. This is the result of increase in recidivism for so many ex-offenders.

So back to square one—the rehabilitation agenda is apparently failing to keep the ex-offenders safely as common citizens in the community. More than ever before, the need for a strong rehabilitation agenda geared on the premises of ex-offender's individual needs could not be overemphasised. At present time of economic downturn and social unrest, the number of crime and the prisoners are increasing exponentially. The government is proposing to build supermax prisons to hold about 2,000 prisoners, like those in the USA. Our prison population is pushing towards 90,000, and the problem of prison management has become more complex, and the rehabilitation agenda in the probation system has become inadequate to cope. Complementary offender management based on restorative justice system has become increasingly more important.

Homicide in Philadelphia: Incarceration in London

Opolu is another young man of 31 doing time in this prison. He loves fast life, fast cars, and high-class living. He cannot remember his parents and was brought up in an orphanage. Life in the orphanage was unbearable for him because of his expectation of a better life. When he was about 12, he absconded from the orphanage in New York and fled away to Philadelphia. He told me that he found his long-expected city where he could live his dream by becoming a gang member. So he started his criminal career in Killadelphia, as it is known now. He also started taking all types of drugs and dealing in drugs to amass a vast capital in as short a time as possible. Opolu carried out his criminal activities at night, always fully armed with pistols and knives. The gang targeted very rich people's houses, banks, post offices, and the street ATMs. Their earning was high at the cost of high risks at all times. Their life was at the hands of the police. Opolu must have been a clever gang member to escape arrest from the federal police for many years. He said many a time it was almost touch-and-go. In a city bustling with gang activities and crimes of all colours, Opolu still remained free to carry on in the pursuit of living a high life as a drug dealer and a criminal gang member.

As it happened, he told me, in a bungled robbery in suburban Philadelphia, he had to shoot a policeman who was about to capture him in that act. Soon he fled from the place and went into hiding. He did not tell me whether he had any family and children. With the help of other friends, he managed to escape from Philadelphia and ended up in London. Time passed by; he had moved from one guest house to another, one area to another, and looked for opportunities to get involved with London gangs. Meanwhile, London Met got all the information about him and the homicide he committed in Philadelphia. The police found out that he was in London and mobilised the force to arrest him as soon as possible because of the nature of the offence that Opolu committed in the United States. The police net closed in, and he was arrested in a street in Brixton while Opolu was selling class-A drug. His trial took place in London. That is how he was in a London prison, serving a life sentence. After four years at this prison, Opolu was extradited to New York to serve his remaining term. We know that American federal law suggests that a life sentence means life, and he would have to remain behind bars for the rest of his life. However, I do not know and will never know whether Opolu was considered for parole at all.

Opolu is smart, polite, and very intelligent. His pottery work has been awarded first prize in a pan-London competition, his artwork has been highly acclaimed, and his written articles have been awarded high recommendation. He has no hesitation in telling me his criminal story stained with hyperviolent past. He chose to follow the criminal career solely because of his ambition to live a rich lifestyle. Perhaps he hated his childhood, being brought up in an orphanage, perhaps he was angry with his unknown mother and father, and perhaps he did not want to accept depravity at its face value. He wanted to build a life for himself devoid of poverty and hunger, controlled by his own motivation. He wanted a life in which he could bury the past, which was embroiled with abandonment, neglect, and oppression. Given his intelligence, he had choices—choices which could have taken him towards a legal career pathway. Instead, Opolu chose the illegal pathway and entered into the criminal world. He does not regret his action, most possibly because the violent criminal career is his own making; no one is to blame. He wants to claim it. He is strong in his opinion and positive in his outlook even with the bleakest sentence he is serving. He reads books on sociology, philosophy, and mathematics avidly, writes short stories in an uncanny way in which you can almost see his criminal past described in colourful beads of words strung together. The stories invariably contain the theme of gang culture, why it exists, and how it survives over the centuries. Occasionally, the existence of criminal gangs has been portrayed as a necessary social evil to protect certain groups of people.

His first-class pottery work finds the prime position in the governor's office. He has completed the Enhanced Thinking Skills course. He has been working as a listener for almost two years, offering advice and support to other inmates who are in need. He has been a member of the education subcommittee for the welfare of the inmates.

There is no doubt he deserves the sentence he was given as a result of his appalling crime. He killed a serving police officer in his call of duty. He took away the life of a human being, a father and a husband. A wife had been made a widow; the children were made fatherless. As an intelligent person, he knows the consequence of shooting a person dead. He also knows that his criminal career was riddled with risks and he might lose his life at any moment. In so far as his offending nature is concerned, it was cruel, selfish, accentuated by the flame of greed. His whole life had been based on selfish intent, aggravated power and domination, and indulgence in high living. Subtract all these evil attributes from his life, you will see a human being of high level of intelligence, willing to accept highs and lows and confident of supporting and helping others.

So what went wrong for this young man of promise? He could not find the orphanage a healthy refuge in which to grow up as a child without parents. Does the society have a part in driving this child into the frightfully unknown and notoriously infamous world of gangs in Philadelphia? The society has failed to nurture the homeless and parentless child to be brought up as a normal child should. In other words, the society has driven the child to fend for himself, being oblivious of his immediate physical, mental, and emotional needs. This is depravity, not created by the child but acquired from the negligence of his parents and, most importantly, of the society. Therefore, without getting to bottom of the critical criminogenic factors, the problem of offenders in the making cannot be solved.

Yours in love

Pumor took me to the corner of the room and told me in a quiet voice whether I could offer him some favour. Pumor is 25, first time in prison, a bit shaky. He wanted me to write a letter to his girlfriend, Sam. He could read a little but couldn't write well. Pumor would dictate and I should write. That was the agreement.

Oh, why is he in prison? He was found in possession of an offensive weapon, a shotgun, in the street of Peckham. He is currently in custody. His case will be heard in six weeks' time. His girlfriend did not know that he went out to Peckham at night with a shotgun. After his arrest, he was sent straight to prison because of the severity of the offence. This was what Pumor told me to write to Sam:

My dearest Sam,

I know you will be surprised and perhaps angry with me because I am writing this letter from a prison. I love you so much. When I went out to Peckham that night, I did not like to mention it to you. I do not like to see you upset.

I'm on remand now, and the court visit will be in six weeks' time. I am keeping my fingers crossed that I would be acquitted with perhaps some community services. After that I will be able to see you and take you out once again. I miss you very much and can't wait for the day when I can give you a hug and a kiss. I hope you have the same feelings for me although I'm in prison. I do miss you badly. I also think about my mum and dad in Croydon. I bet they would be very sad hearing about my situation.

I promise I'll not do this again for your sake. It was my friend who told me to meet him at Peckham. He escaped arrest, running away, and unfortunately I was caught. I hope you will wait for me with tender thoughts until we are together. Remember we were talking about our marriage sometime before. Once I am out of prison, we will finalise everything about our wedding. Please go to my mum and dad and assure them that I'll be out of prison soon to meet with them. Please pass my love to my mum and dad too.

Before my trial date, you all can come and visit me in the prison. I will fill up the visit forms and request visit from you, Mum, and Dad. Once finalised, I'll let you know.

I can't wait to see you all in the prison.

Yours in love,
Pumor

'Binanda, could you please write PS.'

'OK.'

PS: This letter was written by a nice Indian gentleman in the education department. He's cool.

Pumor is an inmate on remand who has literacy and numeracy needs. Although he was sent to school, he did not take school seriously and couldn't do well in any of his subjects. He got bored of schools and preferred to hang around with his peers in street corners with occasional stealing and mugging. His parents could not help him with his schoolwork because they did not have education either. They live on social benefits.

Pumor left his home and shared a flat with another of his friends. Both of them were living on housing benefit and job seeker's allowance. He told me that he met Sam in a gym which he used to visit and where Sam was working. Their friendship grew, and they have been going out for the last two years. Without the knowledge of Sam, Pumor had a darker and weaker side. That is, he goes out with his friends with guns and knives to steal, mug, and rob.

Statistics show that almost 50 per cent of the prisoners do not have the standard of literacy and numeracy equivalent to those students taking foundation level GCSE in British schools. Pumor is one of them. This also highlights the fact that the society is failing in providing inclusive education so that all children are carefully monitored about their basic education and given appropriate support. Children like Pumor are neglected, rejected, and forgotten kids. Schools can be a daunting place for some children with learning difficulties, physical disabilities, and mental impairment. Even able-bodied children face horrendous experience of bullying, abuse, and torture of one kind or another. No wonder then that some weaker children will take the decision to leave school and wander away. Who is responsible for this abandonment? Who is responsible for their well-being?

If we do not know about them, we are, in a way, responsible for their offending behaviour. Putting the blame on their parents, brushing the problem under the carpet, cannot be a solution. Some parents have their own social, mental, and financial problem. Some parents have problems with the police and the law to sort out. Government has a great stake on these abandoned children as a matter of urgency if it is to tackle knife crime and gang violence. These abandoned children will jump at any opportunity to find hope, love, and a sense of purpose. Nobody can deny the potential, skills, and energy that these children have. Abandoning them without trying to understand them, neglecting them without addressing their individual needs, and passing the buck to someone else is to demonstrate the inadequacy of the system of education and training for all young people.

Formation of a gang is the result of grouping of like-minded youths who have lost their hope of living like a normal person. They have nowhere to go for any advice, guidance, and support. They have so many needs, but there is no one to care, no one to support, no one to give them direction. To start with, they do not know the word 'love' from anyone, because there is none who can give them love and care. They have emotional, educational, financial, and personal development needs. But there is no one to see to their needs. Helpless, abandoned, neglected, abused, deprived, and oppressed, these young people are desperate in finding a way out for their daily survival. The result is, a bubble of negative energy concealed in them bursts out in the form of violent act of criminal activity. Nobody condones their act of violence. Equally, nobody can forcefully deny their right to live as human beings and that society has an important part to play for the type of life they are living now. This is a socially constructed phenomenon inherent in the society due to the inequality that exists throughout the ages. Fundamental to the solution is to understand the needs of each and every child. You cannot just leave the entire burden of raising a child with potential problems to the parents alone. It is getting more acute a problem with the rise of lone-parent families. It is therefore a social problem which needs careful consideration and intervention of the government. Removing the root causes of social inequality and depravity will minimise the number of juvenile offenders and, hence, the culture of knife-and-gun violence.

As I am writing this, ITV News shows that in certain areas of the UK 47 per cent of the children are in families who are living below the acceptable poverty level. The acceptable poverty level is measured as 60 per cent of the average per capita earnings of a worker in the UK. The report shows that Manchester came at the top, followed by Belfast, then by Glasgow East in terms of child poverty. No wonder then, without any statistical calculation, we can infer child poverty is a potent factor of street crime, knife attacks, and gang culture. Any government should take a bold step to remove child poverty as a measure to uproot inequality in our society and, hence, to minimise juvenile delinquency, which, after all, is the precursor for adult offending. Leaving such a large proportion of children in unloved, unmissed, helpless, and abandoned state in a welfare society is not only unfair but unjust.

Why am I delving into child poverty in twenty-first century Britain? I thought I was talking about prisons and prisoners to you. Quite honestly though, without talking about abuse, depravity, lack of education, lack of love and affection, lack of moral values in the early childhood, we can't even start a debate on juvenile delinquency. As long as social and economic divide in the state openly exists, as long as the personal and emotional needs of a person remain unfulfilled, offending behaviour of youths will simmer in them and eventually erupt time and again like the unforgettable violent riot that took London by surprise on 6 August 2011. This is what I term the bubble theory of sociology of riots and gang violence. As it emerged from the investigation report, more than 60 per cent of the rioters were ex-offenders. This showed they did not get the help and support for their rehabilitation programme from the probation and correctional social sector. The bubbles of dissatisfaction and anger at the increase in higher education fees and government's cut in the public sector resulting in redundancies and job losses, closure of many high-street shops, and drop in higher education applicants drove the other 40 per cent to join the rioters to take the law into their own hands. Illegal, unforgivable, and callous act of the rioters shocked every citizen of the country. In terms of media language, it can be termed as London Spring. When some of the rioters were interviewed on television, such was the dissatisfaction bubble against treatment of the police, against government's austerity measures, and against the social policies affecting them they publicly stated they would do the same if things were not put right. Understanding their side of the story, what led them to embark on a violent act of destruction of public and private properties of such a horrific scale will only bring some hope of solving some of the inner-city youth problems.

In this prison, in one cell you will find a father and his son convicted of the same crime—robbery. The father trained his son, I was told. In another cell there are two brothers, 40 and 42, from Wales, serving many years behind bars for their part in gang violence and armed robbery. Nobody can open the cell of the two brothers without blocking their nostrils because of the obnoxious smell that prevails in the cell. They live a very dirty life without any showers for weeks and on, smoking heavily all day long and keeping the cell dark. Perhaps they don't like to face anybody because of their criminal activities, or perhaps they think someone might harm them. However, they are kept locked for almost twenty-two hours a day as vulnerable prisoners for their own safety. When they were transferred, their cell had to be fumigated before the cell could be assigned to other inmates. If you walk down to another wing, you will meet two policemen in the same cell. Why are they there? The upholders of law and order are in prison for breaking the law for whatever the reasons may be. Walk down through the playground to yet another wing, and you will meet an uncle and a nephew together in a cell. They are serving time for forgery and money laundering. So criminality seems to run in families. It may not be, however, axiomatic.

Guns, guns, and more guns

He is a Northerner. He is Quas, now 52, lonely, unmarried, with a quiet personality. I wondered why this person is serving a life sentence. On that particular day, he was just sitting opposite me across a small desk. I opened the conversation: 'How did you learn to read and write? What about your parents?'

'It's bad time I gave up my career, I mean the criminal career. I have been at it for such a long time! My father told me to join his business when I was only 8. He did not send me to school at all. Instead, he explained to me how he ran his business of importing and exporting guns. He explained how exciting the business was. I could travel to different countries, meet varieties of clients, see the world, see how the other halves live, and above all earn, enough money to retire at 35. When he drove around the country, I looked at the road signs and began to match words with sounds and began to increase my stock of words to be used. He showed me how he bought shotguns and pistols in black market and sold to clients in other parts of Britain. They in turn sell to clients from the continent at a higher price. We crossed the channel many, many times, many a time with guns hidden in various ways, pulling wools over the eyes of the police. My father even took me to America. We visited New York, Philadelphia, Boston, and Florida. Make no mistake, they were all in business connections. I never saw my mum. I never knew how she looked like. I wish I did. I grew up without my mum's love. Dad cared for me, and that's why he wanted me to be rich like him, doing the same criminal business.

'We have two houses, one bungalow in Yorkshire and the other bungalow in Belfast. We lived a very exciting and risky lifestyle. In one of our trips with guns in our possession, the police finally caught us at Dover five years ago. My dad is still alive in another prison. I'll be transferred to another prison very soon. Quite honestly, Binanda, I feel tired of my life. It is too late to cry over spilt milk though!

'Now give me ten words written on a piece of paper. I'll memorise them in five minutes in the order you give me.'

I obliged. 'Here you are, you have ten words to memorise in five minutes.'

Surprisingly, Quas remembered every word in the order I wrote. When I asked how he memorised each word and in order of appearance, he explained that he associated each word with some of his memorable sentences, until all the words have associated sentences. From the sentences, he then created ten different letters which provided him the order. It was very interesting to see how an uneducated person worked out the way to learn and memorise. No wonder he is now the top student in computing.

There is no doubt there is sufficient remorse in Quas's conscience now. You can just feel how he grew up bereft of motherly love, family affection, and the normal process of childhood life. His father was a lifelong criminal who made Quas a crime buddy. I couldn't see any way that he could have escaped his father's criminal grip. This is transgenerational crime theory. The father wanted to pass on his criminal and risky activity to his son so that the business perpetuates and is in the family. But what a heavy price they had to pay in the end. Both of them will have no chance to get even parole. Prisoners like Quas do not live a normal life since they have to live in a hidden world with people with similar criminal character, away from the sight of the police. They did that all their life until they were arrested and sent to prison. Their way of life and criminal career are their own making. But Quas's case is different in that he was poached by his father to join the criminal profession. He is an unfortunate victim of transgenerational crime. He couldn't have refused his father; neither could he have run away at such a young age. However, as an adult, he had the choice to change direction from the criminal pathway. Once he got the taste of the criminal lifestyle, it must have been very hard for him to give up.

Notwithstanding his criminal career, Quas regrets that he spent such a long time of his life in illegal activities only to find himself in prison to spend his leftover life. What a tragedy for a person who missed out on so many aspects of human life for the sake of living a secret, dark, and dangerous lifestyle. He told me he wanted to give up. But it is too late now. He did not tell me whether they have made any arrangement for some of their other pals to continue with their trade. We will never know.

ONCE BITTEN, TWICE SHY

Rooz is a family man. He is 41, lives in Clapham with his wife and two teenage girls. He is a black African by origin. He has been working as a postman for the last five years. He bows to me from twenty yards away, occasionally gives me a hug before he starts to talk. It was the first floor corridor in the Charlie wing. I saw Rooz chatting to some other inmates, laughing and joking. When he saw me, he came forward to meet me. I asked him whether he could talk to me about his offence. He was very willing to talk about why he was in prison.

'I have been a postman for about five years. I get a wage that I find it difficult to manage my family with. So I found a way to get some extra money in my job. When people send parcels of any kind, I open them and sell them to my local store for a small sum of money. I have been selling items like clocks, radios, irons, pens, and wine bottles. I thought I would never be caught as I am a postman myself. Nobody will know it. But one day my boss called me in and told me that some local people were complaining that they did not receive some parcels they were supposed to receive, and some said their parcels sent to their friends and families went missing. Although I denied that I had nothing to do with the missing parcels, I was reported to the police. Then I was arrested and got a custodial sentence. In my trial the judge gave me six months' prison sentence for my criminal offence. That's how I have ended up in here. This is the first time I am in prison, away from my wife and children. I do not like it here because you learn only bad things—who murdered who, who raped so-and-so, how someone shot a policeman and three of them did the gun robbery. It makes you crazy. I can't wait to see the outside world. I would never do this type of offence again. I have another three months to serve here. You do not think I am a hard criminal like the others in this prison, do you? I stole things to make both ends meet.'

'You know now that crime does not pay. Any crime, I mean. When you are released, I do not wish to see you again in this prison. I hope you have learned your lesson and have had the experience of being inside a prison living the life of a prisoner for six months. I wish you well. God bless.' With that, I left Rooz with a heavy heart.

This was five months ago. Today it is another story. In the Golf wing, I happened to see Rooz again. A long bow from a long distance made sure it was Rooz in person. The man with snow-white teeth came nearer and nearer to me. He shook my hands and said, 'I'm sorry, Binanda, I have let you down.

I am back here again for my own weakness and my stealing habit. I messed it all up. I thought my prison life was over when I first served my time here. But it was not to be. On my release, the post office reinstated me in my job. I was ever so surprised that they cared for me and my family. I am very grateful to them. I was warned, however. I must not try to steal post office properties any more. Else I will have to face the consequences. I must tell you I am not a strong-minded person. Once I started my work, I was looking for nicking any bigger parcel this time. I opened a bigger parcel to find a lot of electronic goods worth a couple of thousand. I began to sell the items again. I did not know that they put surveillance on me. So I was caught within a month. This time I have got a two-year sentence. It only goes to show that I have not been able to get rid of my offending habit. Not only am I sorry for myself, I'm also sorry for my wife and children and for people like you whom I have let down. As I did not listen to the advice of my employer after my first prison term, now I have lost my job, I have a longer sentence to cope with and my future is bleak. Thank you for talking to me. Goodbye.'

Rooz then left, walked to the other end of the long corridor, and mingled with other inmates. I wonder whether he is ever going to learn from his past and give up his offending behaviour. So you see, crime or offending actions take so many different forms that you just cannot put them in one basket—in other words, in a single definition. It is a complex issue whose origin lies in the self and all other criminogenic factors associated with it. In the case of Rooz, seemingly all his needs were met. He had a nice family and a permanent job. He has been paid enough to look after his family and have a happy social life. In spite of having met most of Maslow's hierarchical needs, he couldn't resist the temptation to steal other people's properties because the opportunity to get involved in criminal activities presented itself in the form of his job. There was no peer pressure, there was no child abuse or abandonment, and there was no social and economic deprivation in his case.

His rational thoughts might have been completely blurred or even buried under the powerful lure of colourful crime which would bring him personal financial gain. What is difficult to explain is his committing the same crime again once he was released after his first prison sentence. Another inmate explained to me that it was worthwhile to go to prison on a shorter sentence if the financial gain from the criminal activities is excellent or very good to sacrifice the time lost. He told me in a conversation that unless he could get about £20,000, he would not rob a bank, which he normally carried out with one other gang buddy. Pondering over his first sentence, it is plausible to infer that Rooz might have gained enough money from his criminal act to sacrifice six months of his life behind bars. That obviously bolstered his thought processes with the conviction that crime pays. Blinded by his irrational conviction, he then proceeded to commit his second offence.

We cannot predict whether Rooz will offend again. Perhaps, most likely he will. Unless some correctional intervention in terms of enhanced thinking skills, personal development, and assertiveness is provided to Rooz inside the prison, his attitudinal change might be far away. There is hope for him to change and come to terms with the reality that crime will never pay. With the fact that there is no such thing as a free lunch in any situation, we can confidently say that there is a lot to sacrifice against any criminal act. More importantly, this is an act of human behaviour and deviant motivation for personal gain and gratification. The criminal community represents the darker side of the human mind. It is a fallen community, fallen from the norm of the social set-up. Some of them learn a lot in the prison to turn their life around for good and accept desistance and renewal. Some of them become hard-grafted criminals influenced by the social interaction within the prison and become serial offenders as if to dedicate their lives to a lifelong criminal career.

And on the other hand, some cannot bear the guilt and shame of their action and take their own life in their cell. This is an ugly sight of our society, a sight that almost summarises our frailty, our inability to steer ourselves in the right pathways. There is no denying that we all have strengths and weaknesses and there is a delicate balance between these two dichotomies. Tilt one way, you survive; tilt the other way, you are doomed. Visit a prison, see your fellow humans behind bars, touch a few, hug a few, have conversation with a few. You will soon wonder what has happened to these guys, what has made them commit such horrific crimes, where they have left their loved ones, whom they are against, what they don't like about the other side of the society, and above all, what sacrifices they have paid to be in this condition and if they have got any future to look forward to, if at all.

Come along to the Golf wing, and you will see the drug barons, drug dealers, drug buddies, and drug addicts. You will see humans in the lowest state of health conditions. On Landing 1, look to your left—you will see the long queue for morning methadone. Without that, some of them cannot even pronounce a word. Look to your right: four of them are going to the block because of their misdemeanour in the wing. Go to the Landing 2, someone has barricaded himself in the cell as a dirty protest so he couldn't be transferred to another prison. London boys do not like to move anywhere else in the country, away from their families, friends, and other criminal partners. Open two steel gates to reach the exercise yard. Open two extra gates, and you will arrive at the induction centre. This is a place where the new arrivals are inducted—they are given all the necessary information related with life in a prison. They are given the information on the courses in education department, opportunities to join the workforce, how to apply for a family or a court visit, how to take part in drug-abuse training, how to complain, and how to take part in activities in the chaplain for different denominations.

Induction takes a vital role in opening up the prisoners' eyes as to what it is like to become an inmate. Come out of the induction centre, open another two gates and you will arrive at the Alpha wing. Open another two double doors to enter the ground floor Landing 1. You can hear the banging and shouting on Landing 2 because somebody is protesting since his television has been taken away as a punishment. Further screams and shouting on the top Landing because someone has taken another inmate hostage. Up to nine prison officers are trying to negotiate a deal. Now go to the top Landing corridor. At one end, a group of prisoners are happily having a game of billiards and pools. At the other end, a group of Muslim prisoners are preparing for their morning prayers. You can see one prisoner wearing an overall with blue and yellow squares all over. He is an escapist—he plotted to flee from prison. He needs a prison officer as an escort at all times. On one side of the middle of the long corridor you can see some prisoners having showers. The shower cubicles are only half covered so prison officers can keep an eye on them just in case they try to do something untoward, such as suicide.

That said, suicides are very common in shower cubicles. Peep through the door hole at cell number 233. You may see the inmate sitting on his toilet. If you ask any question, he will answer from that situation. In some cells, they hang a bed sheet or a bath towel to make the toilet somewhat private. Don't forget, most of the cells are shared by two inmates. Twenty years ago, they had to use a big bucket as toilet, which had to be emptied into an outside container to be taken away every day as a ritual. Some of the experienced older prison officers still remember those slurp system days with some dreadful memories.

On Landing 1, you can see two prisoners on wheelchairs. You might wonder why they are in a prison. One of them was shot at in a gun robbery. He was involved in five bank robberies. The other inmate has no strength to walk. He is riddled with the effect of so many medicine prescribed for his pain in his spine. His spine was hit from behind in a knife attack. He is a gangster from Manchester. Both of them are serving indefinite life sentence for public protection. Look at the man in front of you. He has only one arm. The other arm was blown away by a bullet. You can see another one over there; he has a huge bullet effect on his bald patch which looks like a solid block. What about the inmate sweeping the floor? He has a huge slash mark on his left cheek—the result of a horrific knife attack. Go to the Delta wing where you will meet the inmates with mental health problems. Most of them may be in their beds under the influence of the medicines. Some others may just walk about on the floor talking to themselves, perhaps in a different world of their own. You may find a few who have slashed their arms and often cheeks in frustration and anger.

The others may be just screaming in a foul language at the prison officers. Come out of the Delta wing, open two other steel gates and a double door, and you will arrive at the Charlie wing. As you have seen a few wings, you will find some familiarity in the wing. Now take the stairs; open the gates up to the top landing. You can feel the deadly silence at this time. All the inmates are in their cells. These are the vulnerable prisoners on Rule 45. They are at risk of being harmed by other inmates because of their violent crimes. For their own safety, they are usually banged up 22/7, leaving them with minimum association time.

You can now come out to go to the Bravo wing. On your way, opposite the netted playground, you can see many prison staff are having their well-earned puffs in their break in a netted room we call the cage. The whole prison is a smoke-free zone. All officials are required to go to the cage if they want to enjoy a smoke. For the prisoners, however, they are not allowed to smoke anywhere else except in their cell. Well, at least officially. A few gates later, you arrive at the Bravo wing. The set-up is similar to and the atmosphere is same as the other wings. But come with me and open the double gate on landing 1. You will end up at the segregation unit—they call it a block. All prisoners not conforming to the prison rules and regulations, causing grievous or actual bodily harm to others, holding other inmates hostage in their cells, attempting to commit suicide, and abusing prison officers end up in the block. They are banged up 24/7 in single cells, and their movements are monitored. They have to go through the adjudication procedure with the governor in the chair. Usually they get loss of earned privileges, and more often than not, they get extra days added to their sentence if their action is severe. They stay in the block until they are risk assessed and found safe enough to be housed in their cells in the wings.

I hope you are not tired of visiting different wings. Do you find it fascinating and intriguing? A prison is made for the safekeeping of the inmates. The prison governor is wholly responsible for the safety of each prisoner, and he has to recruit highly trained, responsible, and trusted prison staff to run the prison like clockwork. If you now come out of the back gate of the Alpha wing, after passing another three security gates, you will end up in an extended area. On your left is the new state-of-the-art kitchen. The house in front has the accommodation for the IT department and the health and safety department. On your left is the very busy and highly secured security department. They carry out random and spot checks on all workers without any notice. If you now follow the track back and come out of the corridor from the adjoining Alpha and Bravo wings, you will enter the hospital area leading to the education department. We have almost finished, only a few breaths away. The Round House in front of the main gate houses the administrative department, including finance. A few yards in front of Round House, there situated is the governor's office. The governor holds a regular 9 a.m. meeting in the boardroom to take stock of all the activities that took place the previous day and to set the fresh agenda for the ensuing day.

This is your 'tour de la prison', just to give you an idea about the sheer vastness of even a medium-sized British prison. With over 200 officials working inside the prison, the whole estate accommodates over a thousand people on average in any working day. Imagine now, the whole estate is surrounded by a brick-built perimeter wall of some thirty feet high on top of which you will see the shiny razor-sharp blades of steel wire spirals to remind everybody that it is a highly secured area housing some of the notorious and violent inmates in the land. For some it is a frightening place to think about. For others, they cringe at the mention of a prison because of the intimidating feel that it bears. One of the employees called it a day having been in the education department for only about two hours in one morning on her first day at work. On her way to the classroom, she fainted on the first Landing after the first flight of stairs. She did not even get to see her classroom, let alone her students. She was escorted out of the prison, and she didn't return for her job.

SCIENTIST INMATE WHO NEVER GAVE UP

Silo is a scientist from Rumania. He worked at a technical college in Rumania as a lecturer in maths and physics. He came to England on a working holiday and was employed in a factory in Folkestone where he had to use forklift machines in moving big cardboard boxes of cargo. On a particular morning shift, police raided the factory on a tip-off that some people were doing business in drug dealing. During the raid, Silo was arrested together with three other fellow workers on the suspicion of illegal drug dealing. It was alleged that Silo was using a pair of gloves in order that his fingerprints would not be revealed. They were brought to a magistrate's court in London, and eventually, all of them were given custodial sentences pending trials. That's how Silo had arrived at this prison.

He is always smart and well dressed, extremely good in expressive art and computing. When I first met him, he told me, 'I am very unhappy here because I am not guilty of the alleged offence. I was not involved in drug dealing. As a requirement of health and safety measures at my work, I had to use gloves because I was handling forklift machines. But the police had interpreted the use of gloves as to conceal my fingerprints. I have written to the Home Office explaining my innocence, and I am going to represent myself in my trial. I have no faith in some of these barristers. Many a time, they seem to collaborate with the prosecuting barristers to make a compromise that suit them rather than doing what is justice. I am reading the law books in the library, making notes and doing a thorough research of similar cases and preparing my own defence. I am making a folder collecting all the points for my defence together. I cannot wait for the date of my court appearance. I want to prove that I am innocent and have been kept in custody without any concrete evidence. Once I have been acquitted, I'll go back to Rumania to resume my teaching career. I don't like to live in England.'

Silo made quite an impression in the art department. He completed a 12 × 6 ft watercolour of Tony Blair and twelve of his cabinet ministers in canvas as a caricature of the picture Jesus and the twelve disciples. It impressed the judges to claim the first prize in terms of money in an art competition. As to his scientific knowledge, he showed his competence by completing a scientific paper on how to improve the efficiency of a four-stroke engine by using diagrams and complicated mathematics. That was also presented to the competition in the category of prisoners' written work. The paper got high level of commendation too.

Silo has been in custody for about nine months, and his date for court appearance has been fixed. The trial will run for about six to eight weeks. He has got his dark suit dry-cleaned, shirts washed and ironed, shoes freshly polished, and got a few matching ties ready. When the trial started, we could see Silo going to the court with other inmates in the prison van. He stood out as a gentleman, sophisticated and polished and well groomed. With his beard trimmed short, he really looked very smart. In each of his visits, he dressed immaculately and kept his cool and composure. He looked very thoughtful, occasionally worried, downhearted, and exhausted as the trial wore on. The judge summarised the hearing after six weeks and gave direction to the jury in order that they could come to a unanimous decision.

Silo heaved a sigh of relief and pondered over his own arguments for his defence. His mind told him he had done enough, and his conscience quivered whether that was enough to acquit him of the alleged offence. For a moment Silo became angry with himself, why he had to go through the ordeal. For the time being, however, he silently prayed for his acquittal. The trial was over, and the jury returned to the court to give their verdict. You could hear the butterfly fluttering in Silo's tummy from a few yards. He flushed, sweated, and bowed his head.

At the request of the judge, the spokesperson from the jury stood and declared the unanimous verdict that Silo was not guilty of the alleged offence. Silo jumped up from his seat and said loudly, 'Thank you, Your Honour, thank you, members of the jury, thank you, Lord.' He left the court—a free man, declared not guilty, confident of his ability, satisfied with his defence arguments, and proud of his integrity. The following morning was a new morning for Silo—a morning with perfect brightness accompanied by a blue hanging sky overhead. He could smell the air powered by the fragrance of the daffodils, hyacinths, and crocuses in early London spring which he never experienced before. He was out of the prison cell and into the enormous expanse of the outside world where he truly belonged. He has never felt so free, so calm in his entire life. He felt he could hug and kiss the new freedom in his life. He has found a new and deeper meaning of freedom—freedom that makes you 'to be' and feel what you really are. He was going to arrange his return flight to Rumania as soon as he could. He couldn't just wait to see the back of England and to see the faces of all those who were waiting for his arrival in Rumania.

We have no information of the other arrested people with Silo. We also do no not know whether they were all involved in illegal drug trading. Since the initial judge decided to send them to penitentiary, it could be inferred that there must have been such business running in that factory. Silo could have been acquitted, but the very fact that he was kept in custody for almost a year leads us to believe it was a serious drug dealing offence. Silo took the prison custody positively and kept his head up, working towards his defence. Prison life could not get the better of him, although he had to conform to the same routine as any other inmate.

DRUG DRAGON'S DILEMMA

Turo is from down under serving twelve years for possession of cocaine, a class A drug, and for doing business with drugs. He has already been in this prison for the last four years. He is a very polite and kind person of 42. He does not give away much, never talks about his past. Like other conformist inmates, Turo has a great rapport with tutors, doctors, prison officers, and the governor. It is well known that drug smuggling and getting involved in dealing in drugs warrants a hefty prison sentence. That's exactly what happened to my client Turo. As an intelligent person coming from Australia, he made friends with quite a number of other English and Australian people who were also in the business of making a fortune in as short a period of time as possible. They all got together, discussed, planned, and executed their business proposals in importing and exporting large quantities of class A drugs worth millions. They also had a wide business base in London from which they could distribute their illegal catch to big cities in the UK and the continent.

As you can imagine, taking part in such a risky business, you need to be well informed, alert, and ready to change to plan B when required like a flash of lightning. So these guys were not only intelligent and enterprising but also daredevil in their plan of execution. In one particular encounter with me, Turo told me, 'As long as our business was running smoothly, a large amount of cash coming in every week, we have sufficient clients in our network, and we were out of sight from police activities, we all were happy as a lark and felt we were at the mountaintop. But the risk was very high in that some of our clients had guns for their own safety because they had to deal with some dangerous drug addicts and gangsters. We all knew our business was on a knife-edge. However, the power of amassing a large amount of money, the adrenaline rush that flows through us in getting our plans executed, and the feeling of enormous self-contentment in having wealth were overwhelming to keep our criminal activities going. We were living in a secret world—a world in which the actors are the drug dealers, the drug addicts, the gangsters, and the crooked brokers in between all involved in the elusive scene of money transaction. We were all greedy, greedy for money, for power, for wealth, and for sex, which also played some part in our business, there is no question about it.

'But how far can you run from law and the police? As our network stretched from Birmingham to Belfast, from New York to New Zealand, from London to Luxembourg, and from Manchester to Melbourne, it became obvious that we became vulnerable to be reported to the police by some of our own clients. So it was. Whilst I was about to complete a deal for supply of cocaine to one new client in Manchester in a pub, the inevitable happened. Police moved in and arrested us both and took us to London and put me in custody. I did not know what happened to my client. I wouldn't be surprised if he was a policeman undercover. Now it is all over, the final curtain fell. In my trial I was found guilty of possessing class A drug and attempting to supply drugs. Hence the sentence was harsh. I regret having involved in criminal activities, although I knew the full consequences of such acts. As I was young and ambitious, I did not hesitate to join the other friends in crime without even thinking about what the future would hold. I know I have to serve my full term in prison before I could be released. However, I am in touch with my solicitor to look out for any possibility of release earlier on home curfew that is on electronic tagging. I'm getting fed up of living under these conditions. I'm going bonkers. Quite honestly, I have ruined my life.'

That's Turo, a remorseful person for the exciting criminal lifestyle he used to enjoy. Apart from his association with criminal peers, he did not seem to have any other criminogenic factors which might have driven him to the predicament he is in. It is highly likely that Turo will give up criminal activities after his release, which can be surmised from his remorse and from the correctional interventions he has been going through. He has completed the Short-Duration Programme on drug abuse and the course on Prison Addressing Substance-Related Offences. I sincerely hope that Turo will desist from criminal activities to lead a normal life in the community.

What do you think about this young man? He had all other human needs perfectly met as a juvenile and as a young adult. He could have followed a normal career, living a normal family life like you and me. But in his decision-making, he went wayward because of strong social interaction with other criminal drug dealers. It shows the pitfalls that any weak human being may have to face. Once again greed, money, lifestyle, self-gratification, and social status seem to have dominated Turo's decision process, which prompted him to choose the criminal pathway. Drug abuse and sexual offences are associated with most of the offenders if you happen to analyse some of their case histories. Within the prison set-up, there is illegal drug smuggling on almost a daily basis. As a matter of fact, it is rampant in all prisons wherever they are. Drug abuse and drug dealing is a social disease. Under the influence of drugs, the offenders commit indescribable offences. For acquiring drugs for personal consumption or for selling purposes, the criminals will adopt any means from bank robbery to murder without considering any matter related with humanity. All the gangsters in our cities use drugs to be on high to carry out their criminal enterprise. Many of the drug dealers, drug abusers, and gang leaders are known to the police and, hence, to the government.

But more often than not, no action is taken by the police to arrest them and to re-educate, to re-employ, and to prepare them for a future. Until such events like the London riot in August 2011 ruptures, these people with guns, knives, and drugs carry on with their illegal activities right in the face of the police. Even after such a horrific riot in which London was burning for four days, the police and the government could only say, 'These offenders will face the full force of the law, a lesson has been learned, we will be better prepared in the future.' But the truth of the matter is that millions of pound worth of damage has been done and people have lost their century-old businesses and their homes just because prevention of drug abuse, drug business, and dealing with growing gang culture was neglected or not given priority. Although drug and alcohol have been one of the important criminogenic factors which contribute to recidivism, in my own research in 2010, previous convictions; education, training, and employment; lifestyles and relationships; and thinking and behaviour were found to be the four topmost risk factors in the case of thirty-two ISPP (indefinite sentence for public protection) prisoners studied. Therefore, it emerges that impoverishment and lack of education lead to unemployment, which in turn drives the ex-offenders to recidivate, starting the cycle of criminal activities.

IT IS NOT FAIR

He has spent most of his youth thieving, robbing, and mugging. According to him, it was fun, enjoyable, and above all, they became familiar faces to the police as bad boys in the town. He is Upol, who used to live in South London and used to cover an area from Purley to Brixton. He says the police occasionally fined them, but they had the money from their stealing and mugging to pay off the fine. Moreover, they were known to most of the bus drivers running their buses on Route A23. Sometimes they were let off their fare if they did not have any. It's also interesting to note that they used to live on churches' charities. Upol would start the day with his pals in Purley, with morning breakfast at Christ Church, then jump onto the bus to go to Croydon. After doing some of their usual stealing and mugging, they would jump onto another bus again heading towards Streatham. They then would have a hearty lunch at St Andrew's Church, Streatham. Afterwards they would head off towards Brixton to carry out some more afternoon criminal activities before they returned to Christ Church in Purley in the evening where they had to be there by 10 p.m. if they needed any accommodation. If they were there on time, they were offered a hot cup of soup.

Upol is now 38, without any permanent home or any job. He depends on the income from his illegal activities only. Until now he has been in and out of prison for five times for minor offences, with a maximum sentence of six months. Because of his petty crimes from his childhood and his familiarity with the police, prison has become a way of life for him. I have seen him in three different stints in this prison. When I met him again this time, I asked him what he had been in for this time. His whole face was swollen, his eyes were almost hidden under the swelling, and both of his hands were bruised.

Taking a long breath, he told me, 'Hey, Mambwa [that's what he calls me] it ain't fair. It ain't fair at all. I just wanted a few bottles of wine to celebrate my birthday. Since I cannot afford myself, I popped into the local Tesco, begged four bottles of wine, and tried to sneak out. Do you know, when I came out, six security men caught hold of me and fisted me from all sides as I tried to run away from them. It ain't fair. I was one and them six. It's so painful for me, aches and pain all over my body. All I did was taking a few bottles of wine to celebrate my birthday with my friends. But they battered me and handed me over to the police. And here I am again. I have been given four months this time. It ain't fair. All of them know I don't have anything, no job, no house, no money, and no family. They don't do anything to train me for a job or give me a flat to live in. How do I survive? So I carry on doing the same illegal things over and over again. This has been the story of my life. I cannot see a way out of my predicament. It's good to see you again, Mambwa, with that usual smile. God bless you. See you later.'

I left him in his own thoughts to chew over. Do you think he told me the truth? Perhaps yes because he has been a petty thief all his life. He has been a recidivist, a victim of his circumstances which is beyond his control. Upol is a typical prisoner for whom the prison is his escape route for some peace and enjoyment for a few months until he is released again. His outside world is more chaotic and uncertain than his prison where he finds safety and some regularity in life. Consider the prison and the probation system as related to Upol. For a petty thief like him, the British CJS is paying about £34,000 per year to keep him behind bars. Is it necessary to spend that amount of public money for a petty criminal? I think not. There are alternative solutions which might help him to get rid of his criminal habit and integrate into the community and reduce reoffending. By putting him in and out of prison for all these years, the system itself has become an agent which contributes to reoffending.

It would have been far better for the CJS to take a firm step in rehabilitating him and help him build a changed life for him. Admittedly, apart from his minor criminal behaviour, Upol is no danger to public life. Here again the weak correctional policies are at play in failing to address the main issues for his offending behaviour. To borrow from the narrations of some inmates I interviewed, some 30 per cent of the inmates should not have been behind bars. They could have been effectively engaged in productive employment which could have contributed to the economy. It is the belief of many an intelligent prisoner that some 30 per cent of the prison budget could have been used in restorative justice, thereby minimising prison population and recidivism. Considering a present population of 88,000 in the UK and a per capita cost of £34,000 per annum, the saving could have amounted to a staggering £879.6 million a year.

A FRIEND OF THE CJS

Viran is an Indian born in Kenya and a British citizen who dreamed of becoming a rich man by the age of 30 by becoming a criminal dealer in gold, silver, and diamond and various other precious gems. He is now 45 and has been in prison for the fourth time. He joined an international gang specialising in breaking into jewellery shops and robbing as much jewellery as possible. Although his base was at Leicester, he had co-robbers all across the UK, the continent, the USA, and India. He admits he had made millions over the years and been living a very wealthy lifestyle. This time he has been in custody for the last four months, and the trial has been going on. He says he has been known to judges in various courts in the UK. The judge addresses him in formal terms. When he told me that, it seemed as if he rather enjoys being in court amongst the judges and the counsels. Perhaps he feels important as a jewellery and precious stone robber, a rich man in prison, known well to the intellectuals like the judges and the barristers. Unlike some other impoverished inmates, perhaps Viran has millions of dollars stacked away in various international banks in various names in different countries. As a criminal black marketeer in expensive jewellery and precious stones, Viran has been roaming around the world creating a vast network of his clients, making a fortune for himself. When he talked to me, he appeared very relaxed, as if to imply prison is not a strange place to him. It is a part of his criminal lifestyle.

He told me he was a little bit worried this time because the court was about to confiscate his properties. If it happens, he would lose a lot. But his lawyer has been working hard to overturn the decision. Suddenly he mentioned that one of his partners in crime had been already released and he had gone on a luxury cruise to the Caribbean. It is apparent that Viran and his criminal partners are hard-core criminals, highly intent on amassing wealth from robbing high-street ornamental jewellers like Ernest Jones and H. Samuels and selling them through other black market dealers. Viran's sentences ranged from two to three years. He stressed that if you lost some eight to ten years of your life in prison and gained one to two million dollars, it must be a worthwhile risk to take. He continued, 'I have been a criminal for a very long time. It's time I should give up. I would like to give up and spend my time with friends and family. I miss my family a lot, especially my mom. She is in her eighties now, and I would dearly like to see her before she passes away. To be frank, I am getting tired of toing and froing between prisons and courts and living with some other violent and nasty inmates. My court hearing is going on. It would last for another four weeks. Then who knows how many years I'm going to get. Whatever happens, I would like to make it my last prison visit. Unless I'm transferred meanwhile, I'll be able to tell you about the decision of the court. Goodbye and God bless.'

Viran did not come of a poor background. He completed his education up to college level. He could have chosen to get a so-called proper job and lead a normal life. Instead, he chose a criminal pathway to lead a life full of risks, uncertainty, and often violence. His deviant actions and thoughts are generated within his mind. It is conceivable that his involvement in stealing and robbing jewellery and precious stones might have been influenced in part by social interaction with other associate partners in crime. Like many other offenders, he succumbed to his self-gratification, power of wealth, and a world of wheeler-dealers. He has done some homework, as he explained, as to his balance sheet and worked out that even at the cost of spending some ten to twelve years in prison, he would be better off financially being in the criminal act. He could then lead a comfortable lifestyle at his later stage. Inmates like Viran would involve friends and other family members to play certain roles in his activities, perhaps getting them all on his side by sharing his criminal catch. They would be behind the scene in supporting Viran in some ways that would help him put his criminal earnings in deposits and investments for him to enjoy when his offending career comes to an end.

His is a well-planned criminal career designed to carry out robbing jewellery and gem shops and avoiding police arrest as long as possible for the benefit of the criminal group. These offenders have no moral or ethical values. They rob goods from business people who are hard-working, law-abiding, and with high moral and social values. These jewellery robbers do not have any rights to take away hard-earned goods from people who have been earning their livelihood by legal means and by the sweat of their labour. It is evident that the deviance is a mind thing, and therefore, it is related with the offender's brain functionality. We have seen murder committed by 10-year-olds in the James Bulger case in England, a 12-year-old girl suffocating a baby to death while babysitting, and the same girl strangling and killing a dog in her grandmother's house in the USA. These examples demonstrate that offending behaviour can transcend any age. There is no doubt, however, that whatever might be the criminogenic factors, it is the mind, and hence the brain, which is potently operating in the criminal activity. Criminogenic factors influence the activity of the brain cells to generate the criminal mindset. All offenders seem to act on a mindset which defies any rational choice. However, behind all their cloak of offending colour, there is a human being hidden underneath. I believe the restoration of the human being in every offender should be given a priority by the criminal justice system in order to minimise crime, criminals, and recidivism.

SEX OFFENDER'S BLIND SPOT

He has been given eleven years for his sexual offence which he committed on his ex-girlfriend. He is a 30-year-old man called Wopp from Bristol serving his time in London. He is such a smooth-talker; butter wouldn't melt in his mouth. A clean-shaven, well-dressed man who doesn't talk much because everybody knows that he is a sex offender as he has been already convicted of his callous and calculated sexual attack on his last girlfriend, Kinty. His story has been published in the national and local press. About two years ago, Kinty dumped him when she came to know Wopp used drugs and he hung around with many other ex-offenders. A proud and belligerent person, Wopp found it very difficult to accept that Kinty could leave a man like him. He became almost paranoid and vowed to take revenge on her. Although Kinty thought the relationship was over, for Wopp it was another matter. He knew where she lived and began to follow her daily routine, looking for an opportunity to corner her in her own apartment. One particular evening while Kinty was out at work, Wopp entered her apartment and waited in her bedroom with a knife in his hand to fulfil his revenge. When Kinty came back from her work, she entered the apartment, went straight to her bedroom only to be grabbed by Wopp at knifepoint. He then raped her violently at knifepoint, tied her hands and legs, taped her mouth and left her naked on her bed. Wopp did not even consider what was going to happen to the girl who was his girlfriend for about a year only a couple of years back. In other words, he left her there for dead.

Wopp left Kinty's apartment and thought to himself he had got his revenge at last and felt self-gratified. When Kinty's mother rang her later in the evening, she didn't get any reply, and she got worried. Immediately she drove to Kinty's apartment only to find her in the most pitiable situation. She then informed the police, who came to the crime scene. Although Kinty was still in a shock because of what had happened to her, she could provide the details of the person responsible for her horrendous ordeal. The police informed the airports and seaports, giving the details of the offender responsible for raping Kinty at knifepoint. The following day the police were able to catch him in Liverpool as he was trying to embark on a ferry to Belfast. Wopp was then brought to a police station in London and was kept in custody, charged with the sexual assault on an innocent girl. He was given a custodial sentence until he appeared for his trial by jury in the Crown Court. Although he was proved to be the sexual offender, Wopp never did admit that he was responsible for the alleged offence. This blind spot remains as if to cover his act of abominable sexual attack on an innocent victim. Nuance research suggests that most of the sexual offenders never admit their offence. They like to put the blame on the victim, claiming that either the act took place with mutual consent or the victim is trying to take revenge on the offender. Put it another way, they say the victim is the culprit victimising the offender. In the case of Wopp, the jury found him guilty as charged unanimously.

I had the opportunity to meet with Wopp one day for a discussion about his first-level psychology course with the Open University. In passing I asked him about his family and education. He then began to speak:

'I was brought up in a dysfunctional family as a matter of fact. My mum and dad both were alcoholic. There was hardly a day passed without any shout or quarrel in our house. I had another younger sister, two years junior to me. Both of us were terrified of our parents. We got beaten black and blue by our parents for any petty mistake that we made. They sent us to the local primary school. My sister and I did as well as could be under the circumstances. However, when I went to secondary school, things seemed to take a different turn. I didn't take much interest in my study, but spent more time with my friends after school, away from my parents. Very often I used to come home late and got beaten as usual. I used to hang around with friends and smoke marijuana. I became rather withdrawn, hated my mum and dad and their alcoholic lifestyle. I couldn't wait to leave home and go somewhere far away. I completed my GCSE with four pass grades and started my A level to study sociology, psychology, and business studies.

'No sooner had I started my A level than I left home and came to London. I did some part-time jobs in supermarkets and pubs which provided me with income to pay for my food and rent. I made a number of friends some were unemployed, some ex-offenders, and some skilled employees. I hung out with some ex-offenders whose stories seemed to attract me more. Things went okay until I met this girl who gave me a lot of hope for the future. She was gem of a girl to be with, full of laughter and life. Little did I know that such a girl could be so vile to put me into the predicament I am in now. I'm sorry I cannot continue any further. My heart is full of hatred and malice for this obnoxious girl who could do so much damage to me who loved her.'

Wopp is an unloved, abandoned, and vulnerable offender outside and inside the prison. Amongst the inmates too, they seem to hate sexual offenders and paedophiles. Wopp has no alternatives but to face the hatred and nastiness of other inmates every day because of his dreadful sexual offence. He is keeping his chin up and taking the prison sentence in a positive spirit. He has completed the anger management course and has started on the psychology course as a long-time project to keep him occupied. He has been put on the vulnerable prisoners' list, his daily movement is carefully monitored lest he is harmed by any other inmates, and he has been watched stringently by the suicide prevention group for any signs of him thinking about taking his own life for his despicable act of sexual violence on an innocent victim. Wopp definitely needs psychological counselling to instil in him positive thinking with a degree of remorse for his inhuman crime. He knows it well that the stigma attached to him will remain forever and his name is in the national sex offenders' list. He goes through depression cycles and has to take strong medication.

Are you still awake? As I am writing Wopp's criminal character, BBC report is just coming in that Derby arsonists Mick Philpott and his wife Mairead have been found guilty of manslaughter of their six children. This is the case of a violent sexual offender who carried out the arson because of his jealousy, revenge, and malicious intent on his ex-the wife, Lisa, who left him because of his uncompromising behaviour towards her. Philpott had several relationships before he married Mairead and then Lisa. Previously, he broke into the house of one of his girlfriends one night and stabbed her violently. When her mother came to see what had happened, he stabbed her too. He was found guilty of grievous bodily harm and was jailed for four years. Prior to the arson at 18 Victory Road, he had two wives under the same roof with eleven children. When Lisa moved out, after a bitter court battle, she got the custody of her children. An embittered and rejected Philpott and Mairead plotted to burn the house with the hope that they could blame Lisa for the arson and claim a bigger house from the council and get custody of Lisa's children. Unfortunately, the most unimaginable plot went horribly wrong, killing their six innocent children on that fateful night.

In his lifetime so far, he has had eighteen children through five different relationships. His attitude to women is one of contempt as described by former Conservative MP Ann Widdecombe when she interviewed him in his house. According to Philpott, women are meant to bear children, look after them and the house. He calls them 'bitch'. His whole life philosophy is one of power, control, self-gratification, selfishness, and greed in every aspect of his activities. When he was interviewed by Jeremy Kyle on his show,

Philpott remarked, 'I will get what I want by one way or the other.' He has been unemployed with eleven children, living in a council house on a benefit of £60,000 a year. He has been in the media highlight for a number of years because of his unusual sordid lifestyle. He openly says he doesn't want to work; it's the duty of the local council to look after his family. Outside his own body and mind, he doesn't want to know how the other society lives. He doesn't like to include him as a citizen of the 'big society'. He cannot accept the fact that he has been scrounging on the welfare system. His selfishness beggars belief.

It has been proved now that Philpott has lived in his own world—a world in which selfishness, pride, and self-gratification are the main ingredients which drive his way of life. He has the same blind spot as Wopp's; he cannot see outside the sphere of his self. Even after his conviction today, on his way out of the Crown Court he remarked, 'It ain't over yet.' Philpott falls into the same category of offenders as Wopp. Interestingly, he committed a similar violent knife attack on his girlfriend as Wopp did on his girlfriend. Philpott has been sentenced to life imprisonment, and Mairead would be behind bars for seventeen years. The way they cut short the lives of six children is inhuman. In the Philpott saga, there was a third person, Paul Mosley, who was also involved in the arson. He has been given seventeen years too.

The date 1 April 2013 will remain as an important day in British politics. The government has implemented the benefit reform bill. Chancellor George Osborne has pointed out that people like Mick Philpott has been abusing the system of welfare society for a long time, costing the taxpayers billions of pounds. It has been reported now that there are many families in the UK who get council housing, tax credit, and disability benefit by giving false information. Then they sublet the council property, live in their own property somewhere else, creaming enough money on rent of the council property. Can you remember now my first client Amos in the prison? He knew several families who rented out their council houses in England and lived high-society lifestyle in Cyprus without the knowledge of the council. These examples of misappropriation of public money are some potent causes which infuriate some people who do not hesitate to offend in order to show their anguish and prevailing unfairness in the benefit system. It is pertinent to point out that prisoners are a breed of people seemingly right to flag out the unfairness, injustice, and inequality which exist in our society today.

Although the juxtaposed question of benefit cheats and the welfare society is open to wider debate, there is no doubt that sex offender and mass murderer

Philpott has severe mental health issues. It can be surmised that Philpott and Mairead are not a representative couple of the thousands of people who are on genuine social benefits. The police and social service departments could have intervened much earlier, which would have saved the lives of six children and minimised much suffering of the women in his life. This is another example of misjudged and deflated risk assessment which resulted in tragic consequences.

How do you feel about my client Wopp now? His sexual assault and rape is one of the worst-rated offences in the history of crimes. By committing such a crime, he has become a pariah in the society, hated by all for his inhumane offence, condemned by all for his cold, callous, and calculated attack, and spurned by all for not showing any remorse or guilt for his criminal act. If we now look from a theological point of view, all human beings are fallible and prone to sin in a materialistic society. Nobody knows what our life course will lead us to moment by moment; we all can fall into our temptations, into power and greed. We cannot maintain the standards for our lives laid down by God, unless of course we allow ourselves to be controlled and led by God for all our daily activities. Even amongst the apparent God-loving people, we have seen so many fall from grace time and again.

History shows incredible failure of human kind to keep up the life standard that God intends for all of us. President Nixon was impeached for his Watergate affair. President Clinton had a rough ride with the Monica Lewinsky affair. In the sixties Cabinet Minister Profumo fell from his high office with his affair with sex service provider Christine Keeler. Recently, so many politicians in England have been found to have misappropriated their finances. Energy Secretary Chris Hune and his ex-wife have been found guilty of lying and perverting the course of justice. Newspaper journalists have been found to lie, bribe, and hack phones, and the list goes on. Some seem to abuse the position of power, some go with their insatiable greed, and others go for self-gratification. Whatever may be the reason, they all fell from the standard that God set and society expects. And they all show how frail and fragile the human behaviour is. We can be certain of being in the right path only when we allow ourselves to be controlled by the Saviour Lord Jesus Christ. Even with serious convictions, a prisoner has the right to live like a human being and should be given the opportunity to integrate into the community when they complete their time in prison. I am sure you are now confused, whether you are with the prisoners or with other offenders which I have mentioned. Please bear with me. I will come back to my prison clients right now.

THE POLISH BOY WHO DOES NOT LIKE TO GROW UP

With the UK being in the European Economic Community, people from Europe could freely come and work here from the time the UK got the membership. The European migrants are all welcome here because many low-paid jobs are grabbed by them, especially in the farming and construction sectors. Many of them have settled here, were educated here, expanded their families and opened up businesses here. Their contribution to the British economy cannot be underestimated. As the influx of migrants continued, there came the added social problems. Unskilled migrants got involved in petty offences like stealing and mugging to serious offences like robbery, GBH, and homicide. In front of me, in a large supermarket, two European youths bagged a couple of pizzas each in their rucksacks and picked up a can of coke each and left the supermarket without paying for the goods. This is just an example of offence they commit every day. Globalization of prison population has brought different problems for prison regime. Foreign inmates have very different needs than those of our local boys. First, they have language problem; they need translators for communication. They also need video links with their families, which often create extra difficulties in terms of security and cost. It is also quite noticeable that they differ in terms of mannerism and the types of offences they commit.

Meet my next inmate friend, Xeno. He is a young man from Poland who has made a habit of coming to the prison over and over again. He is quite bright, jovial, and with a loud mouth. This 28-year-old Pole has been into all kinds of mischief from the time he arrived in England. He wears a proud countenance, speaks loudly, shows off in everything, and looks down on all others. He says he finished college education in Poland but cannot read the question paper in English at GCSE foundation standard. Xeno has been a classic recidivist; once he is released, he is back again within a couple of weeks. Obviously, as a young man he needs money to survive in London, and Xeno has not any time to look for a job. He wants a lot of money without working hard. He is an expert pickpocket, a regular mugger, and occasionally gets involved in breaking in to steal people's possessions. So he is always under the spotlight of the police. He is also very aggressive, easily provoked, and gets engaged in bodily fight. He told me that it is better for him to be in prison than to be outside when he is always in trouble. He has no money, no job, no family, and no real friends. Because of his temperament, he argues and quarrels a lot. He would go to the education library and demand for a Polish newspaper.

As the librarian has no Polish paper on that day, Xeno would blame the department, the librarian, the governor, and the government at the top of his voice. He is an attention-seeker who likes to be the centre of attraction most of the time. The prison officers find it very difficult to make Xeno comply with prison discipline. He would complain about food, canteen, and his cell. He would fight with his co-inmates while forming a queue to get lunch or shout obscene language at a prison officer because he was told to go back to his cell. Many a time he would end up in the block. A few days later, after his adjudication, he would come back to his cell and start his uncontrollable activities.

Xeno is indeed a misfit prisoner. He cannot just accept orders, no matter how much you explain that he is in the wrong. It is in his blood. He has a dilemma. Inside the prison he feels safe but does not like to conform to the prison regime. Outside the prison he would commit paltry offences to get some money for his food. Last time when the police arrested him for shoplifting, he hit the police. Xeno's life is an enigma. He is a perpetual offender for his own sake, for the continuation of his life, as if he has nothing else to do. It seems very childish, but that is what he is. Away from his country and family, he is helpless, hopelessly lacking direction in his life. Surely, as a young person he needs help in accommodation, education, and training in order to build his self-confidence. Without any intervention for his restoration by the prison, probation, and the social services, Xeno will remain a potential financial burden to the government. Our correctional services have an obligation to work out a programme of intervention which will help this young man not to go down to the abyss of offending behaviour. It is a human duty, a social duty, and the duty of the state not for Xeno alone but for all ex-offenders. Are you sympathetic to Xeno? Have you got human compunction for him for the predicament he is in? Are you upbeat about bringing an offender like Xeno to the right pathway? I am—are you?

LIVERPUDLIAN LOVER BOY

It was a bright and sunny June morning when a group of MPhil students from the Department of Criminology, University of Cambridge, under the leadership of Tutor Ben Crewe visited our prison. We organised a group of prisoners of different category and age groups to meet with the Cambridge group in the education department to have a question-and-answer session. The prisoner students were sitting in a circle to face questions from some of the most intelligent postgraduate students of criminology of the country and their tutor Ben Crewe. They seemed to be apprehensive to start with, but as the time passed by, the conversation became relatively livelier, interesting, and noisy. From my notebook, here are some of the typical comprehensive answers to the corresponding questions put forward by different members of the visiting students.

'I started to offend from the age of about 14. I didn't like school at all and couldn't wait to leave school to join some other friends on the street. I smoked marijuana at 16, and by the time I reached 18, I was heavily into taking crack cocaine. We used to steal electronic gadgets, sell them to buy drugs. We carry knives for our own protection because of our risky trade. Last time, I stabbed a man to steal his wallet. As I ran away from the scene, the police caught me, and now I am here serving four years.'

'This is my third visit to prison. Every time I am released, I promise not to commit crime again. But as you know, we are always with our friends with deviant minds and pass our time talking about robbing, buying and selling drugs. Soon you get caught up, you get encouraged to take risk and offend again, knowing full well that we will be caught by the police one day. For me it is difficult to get rid of my habit. That's why I have been in and out of prison so many times until now.'

'My name is Yool. I'm from Liverpool's Toxteth area. For me school is a history I would like to forget. I didn't think that school and education would lead me anywhere. There was no opportunity for people like us in that high-unemployment area. All we know is crime, drugs, violence, and bullying. We are offenders by law, but we are human beings as well. We are made of the same flesh and blood just like you. We are not born with good fortune like some of you, looking at you guys. We are born with poverty, deprivation, and lack of opportunity. People say we have choices. I say we have no choices open to us except to take the illegal pathway for our survival, let alone looking after our parents or helping our brothers and sisters. I feel ashamed, guilty, and embarrassed with the situation I am in. I wish I could change my offending lifestyle just like that.

'I have a lovely girlfriend in Liverpool. We have been in relationship for two years and talking about getting married sometime. But my offending nature brought me away from her. I miss her so much. You are talking about giving up my habit? There is nothing that you could do to change my offending career. At Toxteth we live crime, breathe crime, and do crime. That is my life, as is the life of so many of my friends there. Nobody does anything for us, nobody wants to know how we live, and nobody wants to improve anything for our lives. I will be out in six months after serving my time and will go back to Liverpool again to repeat my offending trade. I cannot see any alternative. I am sorry, what is there in Toxteth to change people like us for the better? We are just abandoned, unmissed, and unloved youths whom the government and the society would love to forget. We are doomed forever from the rest of the society.'

'You are asking why I am in prison. Have you ever been an abandoned child? Have you been brought up as a child by foster carers without the love and affection of your biological parents? Have you ever been starved? Have any of you ever been homeless? Have you ever experienced what it is like to look for food? Have you ever been in the queue for job seeker's allowance? If your answer to all these questions is no, then you can never ever feel the anger and frustration that an offender has to go through before he takes the criminal path. I do not even know who my parents were. I have nobody to direct me in the right path. I am the maker of my own destiny. Sometimes I wonder whether we have any right to live in this world because we represent the dark side of our society. Although we were born in the same process like you all, we didn't have the opportunity to grow up like you. We have become the hated boys in the street, target of the police, spurned by the society. We do not seem to have any other way to survive but to commit crime. We were definitely not born criminals, but circumstances have trapped us in the criminal loop. Simply put, we have no hope of recovery.'

'How is it like to be in prison? It's like losing everything that you have. No matter how rich or poor we are outside, we are all equal inside the prison. We have nothing to call our own. First you have lost your personal freedom. Second you are cut off from all your loved ones. Third you must conform to the regime at all times. This is no life, man. People say we are enjoying our time here in a four-star hotel. This is totally rubbish. We have lost our self-esteem, freedom, and dignity. I do not say that I do not deserve it. We deserve punishment for our crime. In the same token, we are also human beings. You get so frustrated when everything takes such a long time because of security. Our court appearance takes ages before we are sentenced. It seems it is a show that must go on. The curtain never drops.

'The solicitors, barristers, and the judges take their own sweet time prolonging all cases. To me, that's the way they can earn enough money from each case. To arrange a social visit, you have to wait at least a week or two. Canteen is not delivered on time, usually late. To top it all, we live in fear of our life at all times because you may be harmed at any moment by any lunatic inmate who is always looking for a fight. There may be barricade in one wing in protest, shouting to prison officers in the corridor, suicide in another wing, and maybe a hostage taking on Landing 2. You simply cannot take rest peacefully 24/7. Inside the cell you have another inmate to reconcile with no matter what his crime is. The list goes on. I wouldn't recommend prison for anybody.'

'I agree with what my other co-inmates have said about why we are here. But I have to say the prison does its best to look after us. We get three meals a day. We have facilities to watch even flat-screen television, to make our own tea and coffee in our cells, to attend various classes in the education department, to become a part of the workforce and to go to the gym to keep ourselves fit. We have doctors and nurses to look after our health. We can do many things and earn some money to occupy our time here. We are convicted prisoners as a result of our wrongdoings. So we have to accept our sentence and go forward. Unless you are positive about what has brought you to the prison, you will have a hard time coping with prison regime, you will become a cabbage.'

The Cambridge team had a successful discussion with some of the prisoner students. They were quite happy to give opinions about their offending lifestyle and their experience of the prison life. Perhaps they will have the opportunity to reflect on their face-to-face interview with some of Britain's notorious prisoners. Some might change their views on prisoners, some might have found new perspectives to add to the existing criminological theories, and some might have gathered information as to why it is so difficult to desist. My personal feeling is that the Cambridge team has got the strongest message that the prisoners are human too; they have made big mistakes, but they do deserve a chance to repair, retrain, and restore their lives as part of their human rights. Unless prison, probation, and the social service departments take a sympathetic view on the restoration and corrective programmes for the prisoners, the 'reducing reoffending' agenda will remain as stale as it has been for years. In other words, it would be a denial of the prisoners' human rights.

HONOUR KILLING WITHOUT MERCY

Meet my client Zoop, who has been in this prison for the last eight years, convicted and sentenced for life for so-called honour killing. He is now 33, unmarried, comes of a cultured and rich Sikh family from Southall. He does not like to discuss what drove him to commit such a despised crime like honour killing. People from India and Pakistan seem to have carried on with idea that girls must marry with the consent of their parents. Their daughters are not allowed to marry any man they are in love with. Even after hundreds of years the tradition of arranged marriage amongst some families from these countries still persists. These families put great emphasis on religion and family relationship for their prestige and honour to perpetuate for generations rather than the love and happiness of their daughters. Continuation of such traditions has been at the root of honour killing when some girls decide to ignore the advice of their parents to get married to the man they love. The parents would then go all the way to killing their daughters either themselves or by employing a third party to carry out the killing. This is an offence which cannot be put in the same box with many other crimes. The reason of this type of crime lies in family tradition, religion, prestige, and honour. In the twenty-first century it is an inhuman offence to take the life of a daughter in order to keep the family's prestige and honour alive.

In this tragic story, Surdeep was the young lady who had to die for the sake of their family's prestige, honour, ego, and selfishness. She was the eldest of three children in the family. She had one younger sister an younger brother. Surdeep went through the usual schooling process, got her GCSE with flying colours. She then changed her school to take up her A levels in a local sixth-form school. Her parents gave her permission to change school. It was in the sixth form that she fell in love with an English-born Italian student. Paolo was also a very bright student as Surdeep, and both of them were suited to each other in terms of their likes and dislikes and their ambition to go on to do higher education. While Paolo wanted to do engineering, Surdeep wanted to study medicine to become a doctor after the completion of their A levels. Their relationship grew in their sixth form, and Surdeep's parents came to know of the relation from other schoolchildren.

It is a custom in almost all Indian family that their daughters are well protected from any unwanted relationship in their teens until a marriage can be organised for them according to the wishes of the family. I have to revisit Indian history at this point. It takes me back to the days when the separation of India and Pakistan came about after the independence of India in 1947. Soon after their independence, infighting broke out between the Sikhs and the Muslims in the west, and the same thing happened between the Hindus and the Muslims in all other parts of the subcontinent. In the west when the Muslims tried to drive out the Sikhs from their houses, the Sikh elders slaughtered their daughters with their swords lest they ended up in the hands of the Muslims and suffer rape, harm, humiliation and lose their virginity.

Such is the power of their religion and purity in their thoughts that they would not hesitate to take the law in their own hands in order to maintain their religious belief and family tradition. While her family was determined to maintain their Sikh tradition, Surdeep planned to break rank and carried on with her relationship with Paolo. After completion of their A levels, while Surdeep and Paolo were fixed up with their respective universities, Surdeep's father called her in and told her in the strongest of terms that she had to break up the relationship with Paolo because they had found a suitable boy from Birmingham who had agreed to marry her.

Although it was a bolt from the blue for her, she was not surprised that her parents would do that to her. Surdeep was deeply upset and shocked that her parents could sort out her marriage without her consent in the twenty-first century. Paolo and Surdeep continued with their relationship without her parents' permission and secretly got engaged. When her father came to know that, from his informants, he called his family in and told them Surdeep had to be eliminated before the family honour was destroyed. This is where Zoop comes in. As a brother, he had the duty to uphold the family honour. He promised to his father that he would kill Surdeep within two days. One fateful night, he secretly entered Surdeep's room and suffocated her with a pillow to her death. He then put the body in a sack inside the boot of the family car, drove some sixty miles, and dumped the body in the wood. He carried out this unimaginable crime driven only by the fact that family honour must be upheld. It was Paolo who reported to the police about Surdeep's disappearance two days later. A massive police hunt resulted in finding Surdeep's body after about two weeks.

Zoop was found guilty of the cold-blooded murder of his own sister Surdeep. The parents were instrumental in convincing Zoop that it was the duty of the family to uphold the honour of the family. His parents were jailed for six months each for plotting to kill Surdeep. This is a tragic story of a girl whose life was cut short by the fact that her parents did not want her to marry someone against their will. Indeed, Zoop did not even imagine that he had to carry out the indescribable murder of his sister. He carried out the murder for the sake of the family honour, knowing fully well that he would have to pay the price of his horrific crime. He had become a killer, a murderer; he was forced to kill, but he was not born to kill per se. So how can we analyse his offence from criminological perspectives? It is conceivable to think that sometimes circumstances can create situations in which some people can succumb to embrace criminal act in order that an apparent problem can be solved.

That said, Zoop could have said no to his parents' proposal. In fact, his weakness in conviction and of character has played the better part in him doing the unthinkable. He murdered his sister and was prepared to go to prison. Like any other offenders, he knows that he deserved his sentence. He has, therefore, taken the prison life positively, fully conforming to the prison regime, joining the prison workforce, earning some regular money for his canteen, and taking up the course on introduction to counselling. He attends the gym regularly and has been a member of the staff-prisoner committee for a number of years now. He has contributed to the prisoners' needs and development by proposing some practical changes to the regime. The governor was happy to implement some of his ideas. Very soon Zoop would be transferred to the lifers' prison in Wales, where appropriate facilities and activities are available for such prisoners to engage themselves to keep them fit, occupied, and stimulated. One cannot but feel sorry for Zoop, who became the person spending his entire life in prison for the murder he committed for which the only criminological reason is 'family honour'. If he is considered for parole in the distant future, I do not think he would commit such crime again unlike other typical perpetual offenders. Only the future will tell.

I am so glad you have patiently heard the stories of my prisoner clients. These are real people, committing real crimes and serving real sentences in a real prison. These are my close encounters with them, face-to-face. Perhaps you might have hated them all for their offences, perhaps for the amount of public money the government has to spend to keep them off the street for public safety, or perhaps for their very deviant minds and thoughts. But have you considered the fact that they are part of our society? Have you also considered that the prisoner community belongs to the human race, the Homo sapiens, whose ultimate wish is to reach self-fulfilment? So where did they go wrong? And why should they go astray? What are the reasons that they go astray from the common societal goals? Given the fact that they are part of us, haven't we got any obligation to contribute to the restoration of their lives after they have served their time? Are you willing to accept that we are in some way responsible for driving them to despair—depraved, disowned, disaffected, and disillusioned—and to commit crimes?

By us, of course, I mean the criminal justice system, prison, probation, and social services in general and the government in particular. After all, these prisoners were amongst us in the community while they committed the crimes. Many of them are ashamed of their offences, remorseful for their offending career, and willing to change course provided they are given appropriate help, support, and training to lead a normal life. As a matter of fact, given the choice, all prisoners would rather live outside of the prison in the community than to live in a 9 × 7 prison cell. This is overwhelmingly the case, proven by research, showing the human side of a prisoner's life.

I hope you haven't fallen asleep yet! I have got my own research evidence to tell you now. Are you ready to listen? I hope you are. I have given some part of the text of my research work as it appeared in my MSt thesis titled 'Critical

Study of Criminogenic Factors Contributing to Recidivism and their Impact on Policy Decisions' submitted to the University of Cambridge in 2010. It may be somewhat heavy for you, but I do hope you will enjoy hearing it as a part of the bad boys' story.

OFFENDERS' VOICE

Here are some samples of 'voices' from the actors—the key players in this study. It is apparent from the narratives that the actors are 'alive' with comments and experiences imbued in their criminal trajectories which can lend support to certain themes or attributes associated with these offenders as summarised below. I have grouped their commentaries under different headings. Each quote refers to an individual inmate. These voices were captured through face-to-face interview with fifty-two clients who are known to be repeat offenders from prison records.

DESISTANCE ATTRIBUTES: CHANGE IN SELF

'I do not want to come to prison again. I just want to look after my family and stay with the kids and keep away from my peers. Some people like prison, they might reoffend. Some people cannot be helped. You must have faith and belief to desist from crime.'

'Only I can change the state of affair. I need employment and support. I must be careful about whom I associate with. Partner is living in a flat with my little girl of 3 years. They get family support and housing benefit.'

'Move me away from my area. I have drinking problems. My offences are related to alcohol. I'm easily led by others. My mum died when I was 17, and I started to offend. My brother is also an offender. He killed himself by injection when he was 38. I have five brothers and three sisters. All my brothers are offenders. One can give up crime by making a conscious decision.'

EMPLOYMENT AND TRAINING NEEDS: MAJOR NEEDS

'Provide me with more training opportunities, more education about crime, drug, and alcohol. I prefer community sentences as opposed to prison sentence. The police is a major cause for [forcing] reoffending once you are an offender. Also, for some repeat offenders, prison is a safer place.'

'feel disappointment about myself and occasionally feel suicidal. We need education, employment, housing, and counselling about drug and alcohol.'

'If I have to give up crime, relocate me and provide me with housing. Help me to start up a business. On release I'll join with my partner. My reoffending is mainly due to drugs.'

MENTAL HEALTH ATTRIBUTES: REHABILITATION NEEDS

'I have been using drugs since the age of 14. My grandfather was in jail because he was an Irish terrorist. My father was in jail because he was a drug dealer. He left my mum to marry another woman and left me with my grandparents. I took to offending because of death in my family. My sister died when I was 11, and just after that I lost my grandparents within a year. I have taken all kinds of drugs—cocaine, cannabis, and crack. I hate my dad. He is still doing business [drugs]. I first took heroine in this prison. [Looking out the window.] Can you see over there? That's Peckham, which is a shit and where I grew up. Look at my hands, full of knife cuts in street fights. I tried to commit suicide three times. Twice I tried to hang myself, and once I took overdose. I am a bipolar. I go through highs and lows. Once I jumped in front of a bus, and another time I jumped into the Thames. I was in hospital because I broke my knee. You know, Guv, one has to be clean in his heart to be good. I am 29 and have been a criminal all my life. I did not do nothing. I am a licence recall this time. You are a good man. God bless you.'

'I am 40, married and divorced. I was sent to school, but never attended. My father left my mother and went abroad. I left home and lived with my friends with no jobs, no qualifications. We steal things, vandalise cars, and assault the police to get a kick out of our lives. At 30, I was diagnosed schizophrenic, having a split personality. We are known to the police as petty criminals, and so we are in and out of prison many, many times. They release us, nowhere to go. We get together again and commit offence. I want to give it up if I can find a nice woman and somewhere to live. I can find a manual job without much difficulty.'

'I am a gypsy, have been in the business since 5. I am now 42. We are brought up by the roadside and learned to live by stealing and street fighting. No school. We steal goods from people and from supermarkets. I learned some trades—tree surgery, paving, gardening, and barbering. From stealing we started burglary and stealing cars. Then I got involved in gun robbery. This time I stole a police car to do commercial burglary, and there was shooting.

I'm getting tired of doing the same thing and want to give up my habit. But the sight is not near yet. All I need is my driving licence back to do my trade. Then I'll give up. I can have my own earnings then. I have personality disorder, cannot stand still for a moment. I have to move about.'

'I think the prison should be for help not for punishment.'

ACCOMMODATION ATTRIBUTES

'I need a roof over my head, a job and career prospect, a good non-addict friend, and family support.'

'I have no job. I have a girlfriend, and eventually I might marry. As I need money, I commit crime. I can help myself only.'

'I need to smoke five packets of cigarette a day, then I cut down to five packets a week, then two packets a week, and I gave up for three months. Then I started again by mixing up with friends. So, criminal behaviour is very difficult to give up. Criminal activity becomes a habit. You seem to forget your previous sentence and commit another offence, and you get sentenced again because you are already labelled a criminal. You do not have a job, you do not have a house and nowhere to go, except mixing up with other criminals.'

'I have been to prisons innumerable number of times from the age of 13. I take drugs and sell drugs. My offence is mainly theft. I am a pickpocket. I have six children from different women. I never got married. I cannot look after my kids. Grandparents look after them. I genuinely want to give up crime to start a new life. I never had a house. I need a flat. After a while you get fed up. Now I just want to help other criminals who need help in their lives.'

'Instead of locking up for twenty-two years, we should be rehabilitated. Provide housing and [real] jobs. Rehabilitate me to the community. It causes anger and violence in prisons.'

LIFESTYLE ATTRIBUTES: CRIMINALITY BEGETS CRIMINALITY

'I am 35. My parents were drug takers and drug dealers. I did not go to school at all. I just hang around with my friends, and they pressurise me to do things. I have no control of my actions because I was young. My first offence was at 14 for stealing cars. I took drugs at 12 and dealt in drugs for earning money. I never went home as my parents did not want to know me. I have been convicted five times now for drug dealing, robbery, and stealing cars. This is all because I need money to feed my wife and my baby. Drug dealing is my main offence with the intention of getting money to live a lifestyle that I want. Once convicted of one crime, we are always in the eyes of the police, and they will arrest us and send us to prison for any minor offence. So the criminal life cycle continues.'

'My criminal life started in Portugal where I used to live and sell drugs. When I came to England, I started a new life. I was working and engaged in sporting activities. But when I found out that my girlfriend was pregnant and at that time I wasn't working, I needed money quick and easy. That's when I started selling drugs, heroin and crack cocaine. Within a year I had developed a habit of taking hard drugs. I lost my wife, my son, my friends, and my house. I lost my self-esteem, and I lost everything. So I became a criminal to feed my drug habit, from that to commercial burglaries. Anything would do as long as I could get the money to buy drugs. I did not care. After a couple of years I got arrested, and here I am in prison paying my debt to the society. I think if it wasn't for the drugs, I wouldn't have been here. But that's life. I just hope I go out and stay out of drugs, get housing, get a hobby or a job, and change my social life.'

'I have robbed 250 Sun computers so far, each costing around £100,000. I get about £35,000 per computer. I live for money and lifestyle. I also take drugs and deal in drugs. I have assaulted the police two times. I have had fifteen convictions.'

'I am 48. I am from Alabama, no education. I got married to an Englishwoman. So I have been in England for the last ten years. At first my addiction started with alcohol, and then I went on to take with class-A drugs from the age of 22. I have grown-up children and my wife. I started offending from the age of 20 and have many, many offences. It is my habit that I cannot give up. I cannot even provide for the existence of my family. My children also have offending character. They don't have no education, no jobs.

'If I have to give up reoffending, then probably I would have to have the right kind of money to support me and my family. So it is the job I'm looking for. I'm at the age that I wouldn't like to go on reoffending. I'm ready to change my offending habit if only I could have a job.'

SYSTEM ATTRIBUTES: POLICE COERCION

'Some people are not supposed to be here in the first place. So I will say that the system fails them, and they actually learn bad stuff whilst they are in prison. This miscarriage of justice drives people to reoffend. The system is racially biased in the sense that black and Asians are very likely to be arrested and jailed for trivial issues which they harbour and make them reoffend. The prison system is not well equipped to deal with problems which brought the person into prison in the first place. This lack of resources means the offender leaves the prison with no change of heart. Once someone has been jailed before, the police will always assume the person is a persistent offender. Prisoners are locked up for long hours in their cells. Hence they become socially deviant, which can contribute to bad behaviour and reoffending. Things like drug—and alcohol-related issues must be dealt with by well-trained professionals who understand the problems, not the prison. Lastly, the police should be well trained to be able to know which case must go through criminal justice system and which must be referred to professionals.'

'I am searched every day by the police. Because you are black and young, you are a suspect, the police say. I used to smoke heroine since my childhood. My first offence was possession of drugs. I got three months. Then I promised not to be convicted again. Even I went to university. I have now owned a courier business. I earn enough money to look after my family and kids. This time the police caught me while I was taking two ladies to a hairdresser. They stopped me for possession of drugs again. The police always try to get a conviction to show that they are controlling crimes. They have pressurised my wife and my mum to confess that I had the drugs while I was driving the van just to get a conviction. My last offence was seven years ago. No way will I come back to prison again.'

These responses were obtained through face-to-face interviews with the participating inmates in different locations—in the cells, in the playing areas, in wing corridors, in the gym, and in the education department. The above are some captivating statements from some of my participants in the research project. Some are certainly poignant, depicting their inner feelings and the situational contexts in which they get involved in criminal activities. Some remarks are repugnant, without any trace of human sensitivity. Some of them became criminal almost by default—a result of a transgenerational life event. Some others show their helplessness of imprisonment and are pleading for help and support to renew their lives in the normative society. For certain offenders, prison is their only place to go for their survival and safety. They are not equipped with the skills necessary to survive in the outside world. Prison is their coping mode of living a life. One then wonders why prison, probation, and even the Ministry of Justice continue to exist at the cost of all the criticisms, had there been no 'social Darwinism' at work in our society to produce the lawbreakers labelled criminals.

I also conducted fifteen focus groups, each consisting of twelve inmates. The commentary from individual interviews bears similarity with the responses made by the offenders at various focus groups. It emerges from the focus group studies that there are some common threads that link their criminal journey. The groups are heterogeneous in terms of their offence, category, and age. However, most of them come from deprived economic backgrounds and broken families. Neither did they have any fixed abode or any employment at the time of their offence. Prisoners with white-collar crimes seemed to have their own housing and bank balances, while the other groups are desperate to know about the well-being of their families that they looked after from their criminal earnings outside the prison.

These prisoners are not all repeat offenders. Some are in prison because of immigration rule violations. One aspect of the immigration cases is worth mentioning here. Some of the immigrants are released after a few weeks, only to be arrested again because they do not possess the relevant papers, including passports. They are therefore are forced repeat offenders in that they have no power in themselves to reintegrate with the outside community even if they wanted to. All the groups were asked whether they would like to desist from crime or there is any likelihood of their coming back to prison again. In the random sample of 180 prisoners who took part in my focus group studies, 80 per cent said they would like to quit their trade, while 20 per cent of them said that they might have to return to prison for various reasons which were outside their control. These reasons primarily fall under the mental health attributes for recidivism. From these group discussions it can be concluded that social interaction has been a potent correlate of recidivism for most of the repeat offenders.

They believe that only by dissociating from the interaction of their offending associates can they achieve desistance from crime. There is a good deal of rhetoric regarding reducing reoffending and prisoner rehabilitation, but the reality is far from satisfactory. The reoffending rate is on the upward spiral, which shows that the system is not working as planned. The prison and the probation services must put more emphasis on prisoner rehabilitation and employment in order that the very purpose of reducing reoffending is fulfilled.

Well, I have told you the life stories of twenty-six bad boys together with several other offenders thrown in to complement the collection. Perhaps you are getting tired and about to fall asleep. I am very glad that you cared to listen to the inside stories of the fallen community behind bars. Many people do not like to know about their life; they would rather throw the keys away after they are banged up, as if to say they are not our problem any more. Indeed, nobody condones the act of crime. However, crime and criminality are born within our society. As long as our human society exists, so will crime, criminality, and deviant behaviour. We have to accept the culpable nature of human beings as can be seen from the immense number of prisoners from every conceivable walk of life. From the biblical perspectives, sin, rule violation, temptation to go against the law started at the Garden of Eden when Eve, tempted by the sweet word of the serpent, ate the fruit from the tree of wisdom, which God forbade. It is the very sin which permeated through generations after generations. Christians believe that without the shed blood of Jesus Christ, nobody can achieve eternal salvation. That is to say we can be put right with God only through Jesus, who has already paid the price for all our sins and inequities by his death on the cross.

In line with the same argument, from the cradle to the grave, a person needs to be guided to be on the right path first by the parents, then by the school, and then by the state by loving, supporting, guiding, providing, and disciplining where necessary. In one of my deliberations, once I was told by an eminent barrister and president of the Law Society that justice is one thing and law is another. Therefore, there is an apparent mismatch of law on one hand and justice on the other. By putting an offender behind bars, the law protects the public and punishes the offender for his crime. But what happens after the crime and punishment is the central theme this book is trying to address. While the prisoner has paid for the price of his criminal offence, as a human being he has the right to come back to the community to be treated as one of us. Ironically, that is not the case. Their criminal label makes them still vulnerable to be coerced into offending, alienated in the society, despised for their offence, and ostracised at every opportunity that presents itself. That is the time these ex-offenders need help, support, advice, and guidance most to build their broken lives.

EPILOGUE

This has been a long journey and an eye-opening experience. When I started my teaching career, I never even imagined that I would be spending seven years working with prisoners in a real prison estate. I was called in to teach social and life skills temporarily for two weeks. Then I was made permanent after four weeks, first as an outreach tutor, then as a deputy education manager, and finally as a centre manager until my retirement. I was overwhelmed with the wasted lives of so many human beings who have gone astray, morally adrift, emotionally shaken, and spiritually bankrupt.

Inside the prison, their life is an uphill struggle. Never a moment passes by when their heart is not crying out to be outside the wall. Popular belief apart, I did not come across any inmate who would like to spend their time behind the imposing perimeter wall. Even the wall cannot separate them from the outside interaction. The open car park behind the Golf wing is an interesting area where young ladies would come and have chats with their 'bad' boyfriends in their cells. They talk for hours even into the late evenings. People throw drugs over the wall with the hope that the right person inside will get the 'goody' sometime. Drugs are smuggled in by various ingenious ways. Although the security department has eyes like a hawk, mind like a chimp and acts at the speed of light, still drugs and mobile phones creep into the cells without the security department noticing it. You can see that even at their peril of facing the governor's adjudication, all inmates would love to be in contact with the outside world. I was told that most of them carry on with their business and money transaction through banks outside by using their mobile phones.

It just goes to show how much the prisoners miss the outside world and the freedom they used to enjoy. All the prisoners I talked to agree that they have been found guilty of the crime they have committed and, hence, they deserve imprisonment by law. But the life behind bars is not for the faint-hearted. For some inmates prison is a safe place for them to spend their sentence away from the risky world they used to lead outside. For some it is a place to learn more of the illegal activities to become a hardened criminal. For a minority few, prison life and their sentence are unbearable, and they decide to take their own life. Yet there are those who accept the prison life, conform to the prison regime, and look forward to coming out of the prison to lead a normal life in the community.

Working in a prison is a stressful job for all prison staff. All staff work round the clock to make the prison a place of safer custody for the inmates. Due to staff shortages, effective delivery of the regime becomes difficult at times. That is one of the reasons when the inmates are banged up for longer hours for their own safety. All inmates resent when they miss out on their association times, and they become very frustrated. Things have been changing over time. Change management has been in place; prison management has progressed towards a businesslike model. This new penology is based on focussing on targets, managing time and labour, and achieving priority targets on time. This requires efficient and highly skilled prison staff, a progressive governor, and a well-planned, functional services for the benefit of all the inmates. While the present government is proposing a new way to deal with incentives and earned privileges (IEP) for the inmates, in many respects, however, prisoners should be considered for employment and privileges in the prison according to their conformity and cooperation with the prison regime.

My experience suggests that occasionally some services get neglected because booking online has to be made in order to get the work done. This takes time because of the long-windedness of the process. Furthermore, some services are privatised, and it is at the company's mercy which work should be given priority. As the education manager, it was my responsibility to make sure that the department is organised to the highest standard for the effective delivery of the curriculum. As the education department is expected to be the prison's flagship service provider for the inmates, it is extremely important for me that all classrooms, toilets, and landings are kept spotlessly clean. During my time, former Labour Home Secretary Clark, HRH Princess Anne, and postgraduate students of the Criminology Department of the University of Cambridge visited the department. Many a time prison staff, local business people, and prisoners meet in the education department for lively discussions and working out effective strategies for ex-offenders' employment. So I had to be very vigilant at all times for any breach of health and safety requirements.

At a particular time, for about two weeks there were no prison orderlies who cleaned our department before the classes began; they were not available. They got transferred to other prisons. Without proper security clearance, these orderlies could not be appointed. During that time, I used to clean blocked toilets using hot water from an electric kettle and a toilet brush because the smell became almost unbearable. Almost every day I cleaned the classrooms, and on one occasion I swept the whole spiral fire escape which was covered with cigarette butts and other litter. Nobody knew that I kept the department clean myself, because it was my department and I was responsible to have it cleaned. When the workers were not available and there was no alternative to have the department clean and fresh, I decided to do the job myself although it was not in my job description. I could not bear to see an unclean and unhealthy department in which my students could work, be they prisoners or mainstream students. You can now see how difficult it was for me to coordinate my activities in a prison education setting. I also felt there was a culture of passing the buck between the service providers, which prevented getting work done at a quicker pace and in an effective manner.

When I started my job as an outreach tutor and Open University coordinator, I opened the opportunity for the prisoners who could not attend the education department for their vulnerability, ill health, or physical disability by bringing education to the cells for the first time in the history of education in the prison. It was a pioneering effort to provide inclusive education to all prisoners. It was effective, exhilarating, and stimulating. The prisoners who were on Rule 45, those in the medical wing, and those with physical disability and who were wheelchair bound missed out on education before I developed the ICE (In-Cell Education Project). I started with one self-harming prisoner, and within a period of two years, over 100 students were enrolled on the ICE Project programme. The prisoners were provided with material to develop their basic reading and writing skills. Those who were more capable were prepared for Level 1 and Level 2, literacy, and numeracy examinations. Tests were conducted in cell under exam conditions. During a period of seven years, more than 100 prisoners received their Level 1 and Level 2 certificates. Some of them never even imagined that they would hold a certificate in their hands in their life time.

You should have seen the jubilation and jumping with joy when they were delivered the certificates. The ICE Project was highly acclaimed for which I was offered the prestigious Butler Trust Award in 2008. In the mainstream education, a Purpose-Driven Project (PDP) was developed to specifically deliver entry-level literacy to the prisoners in a classroom setting. The project is still going strong after almost ten years. Another project termed Connect245 was developed to provide education to the inmates on Rule 45. Prisoners with experience and qualifications were used to act as coordinators for running the project smoothly. Working closely with Prisoners Education Trust and Good Book Company, grants were arranged for those prisoners who showed competence to follow first—and second-level undergraduate courses with the Open University and certificate-level courses with the National Extension College. Regular examinations at Level 1 and Level 2 are held in literacy and numeracy departments when the students are well prepared to take the exams.

Modular assessments provide further achievements in information communication technology and social and life skills. More qualifications are offered in radio, industrial cleaning, and physical education. Although there is no provision for any qualification, many inmates choose to do the programme in art. This is just a snapshot of some of the education programmes that are open to all prisoners. At one time I provided the training on interview techniques for some prospective prisoners looking for employment as chefs in an international chain of French restaurants. All education programmes are designed and delivered with the specific aim of equipping the prisoners to develop confidence in gaining employment when they leave prison at the end of their sentence.

Social structure and social reproduction will continue for the survival of the human kind. Concomitantly, it would bring social division of inequality, which will bring about disaffected, abandoned, and uncared-for people who will choose to accept the criminal career when there is no other pathway for their livelihood. These people need help, support, and guidance in the early stage of their life. If a strong policy is developed to discover the early deviants and delinquents to provide them with necessary education and life skills, surely most of them will choose to live a normal and productive life. In a recently published literature, our society in England at present has been shown to have three dimensions and, hence, three capitals—social, economic, and cultural. A class is defined in terms of how much of the capitals in each dimension a particular class possesses. According to the study, there are seven classes: elite, established middle class, technical middle class, new affluent working class, technical working class, emergent service workers, and precariat or precarious proletariat.

Although we are now in the twenty-first century, the class structure has proliferated, demonstrating the divisions that the society has created through the annals of history. Therefore, inequality will remain, and the struggle for the precariat to achieve any other class echelon above will be steeper than in any other time before. The resentment of not achieving their ambition, the anguish of being abandoned, the frustration at the uphill struggle lead this group to choose an offending culture. So it is for us to see and explore who could be at the root of the offending culture and what could be done to prevent or minimise the risk of putting them in that situation. Society will prevail for all the time to come, class structure will thrive within society, and crime will never die because it is born in the society, created by the disaffected deviants as a means of their survival.

As the prisoner population is increasing at an alarming rate than ever before, the prison and the probation services are facing a mammoth uphill struggle in the present climate of economic downturn and government's austerity measures in public services. It is my sincere belief that the government would take steps for developing early intervention for the offending community with humane programmes to prevent crime to create a safer society. The bubble theory of sociology of conflict suggests that without taking the preventative measures for removing the causal factors promoting offending behaviour amongst young adults, the unimaginable violent summer riot of 2011 might be simmering for a while and could erupt again without any notice. Then it will be too late, as it was the case for the devastation that resulted in 2011.

Preventative measures are at the root of controlling crime and violence. I experienced schoolboys attempting to hurl a stool at me during a lesson, switching the lights off and playing football at the back of the classroom, and snatching all my teaching materials from my desk within a few minutes of my entrance into the classroom, never to be found again. In that challenging school, the boys jump over the window into the classroom instead of entering by the entrance door when they are late for school. And late they were always. In another school, I had to walk through a big park to reach the school. I was appalled to see young boys and girls sitting down on the grass in groups, smoking and taking drugs. That was before the school started. On my first day, the school was ablaze; the whole library and part of the science block were completely gutted.

This happened to be the action of a group of students. During my one year at that school, there were three cases of arson, there was daily stealing and mugging, and there was police presence almost every day. Yet in another school, some students of year 9 to year 11 smoke marijuana in the toilet and then come to the class. You can immediately smell the waft of marijuana hanging heavy in the big classroom.

These types of young people need real help in terms of their educational and personal development as a special provision. We know these students who have no prospect of gaining any qualification through mainstream education. And there is every possibility of some of these students ending up being gang members, drug dealers, and maybe prolific offenders in the future. You can see now how a criminal career is born in our society. I have seen disenchanted groups of boys hanging out at street corners in Bradford, Leeds, Manchester, Birmingham, and London. These scenes of unemployed, disaffected, and wayward boys, looking for something to do, remind me of the Altgeld boys in Chicago as described so vividly by President Barack Obama in his book *Dreams from My Father*. Altgeld was then a dilapidated housing estate, ironically called the Gardens because there was hardly anything green that bothered to grow there. As a social worker, as he was then, President Obama's heart went out to these kids and their families, and he found it an uphill task because of the impoverished conditions of the schools, churches, and the neighbourhood. So he proposed to start at the grass-roots level of improving the housing, living conditions, schools, and relevant school curriculum. He worked with the head teachers, church leaders, parent-teacher associations, and the local council to help forge his transformation agenda for the community.

I am sorry I had to tell you some of my experiences with young people of England as well as to describe similar youth groups across the pond. I believe they have got relevance in recognising the nature and origin of crime. Crime is, thus, a social problem, a social disease, a social evil. In combating crime and violence, therefore, the whole of our society must be together to develop means, ways, and policies to prevent crime. In that recognition and perception of crime and violence lies the prescription so vitally important for preventing or minimising the chances of crime happening for that matter.

As I am trying to wind up my writing for you, yet another gruesome criminal act committed by two British born and of Nigerian descent has been reported in the BBC news. Michael Adebolajo, 28, and Michael Adebowale, 22, carried out the savage killing of Lee Rigby, 25, a British soldier who served in Afghanistan, on 23 May 2013, near Woolwich barracks in broad daylight in front of many onlookers. These two perpetrators had been known to the police and the British intelligence for several years. Yet they were not treated as a threat to the public. They have now been found to be terrorists with extreme and radicalised religious views. Once again, deterrence and prevention have proved a failure. One innocent man was brutally murdered for the lack of accurate assessment of terror threat. Until now ten other suspects have been arrested in connection with the Woolwich murder. It was also the case for the 7/7 terrorist attack of 2005 when so many people lost their lives. The attackers were known to the British intelligence service for many years prior to the bombing on buses and trains in the City of London. Without accurate risk assessment of ex-offenders or suspected offenders, there will always be crime at large. And there will always be hard lessons to be learned and bitter pills to swallow. After the Woolwich murder, Prime Minister David Cameron and Home Secretary Theresa May have proposed to establish a special task force to study extremism and radicalisation. Although we welcome such an agenda, it is long overdue because that was proposed by the Labour government when they were in the office.

Oh dear, you have fallen asleep, my sweet friend! But I have got so much to say about the prisoners, their violent crimes, their exciting lifestyles, their risky businesses, their drug habits, their emotions, their cries, and their wanton desire to come out of the prison gate to be able to breathe the fresh air and hug their friends and families and be human once again. Maybe I will tell you about their desire to desist and how they can overcome their power to offend sometime in the future.

Good night. Sweet dreams and God bless.

ABOUT THE AUTHOR

Prestigious Butler Trust Keith Bromley Award winner for his outstanding work on education and skills for prisoners in 2008, the author has seven years of experience of working with prisoners, at first as an outreach tutor and finally as a head of education. He holds a master's degree in applied criminology, penology, and management from the University of Cambridge. His teaching career in schools, colleges, and universities spans over thirty years. In this book, he has captured the poignant and sometimes repugnant voices of the prisoner community, from a humanistic viewpoint. Their emotions, elusive world, and expectations inside a prison estate, as they vividly expressed, are presented as a collective story in a simple language to offer a glimpse into the world of prisons and the prisoners. He has also tried to demystify the societal perceptions about prisons and prisoners and why we should endeavour to look at the prisoner community from a more humane perspective if we are to reduce reoffending and reintegrate ex-offenders into our community.

The author sincerely hopes that the book will be helpful for those who would like to have an overview of the day-to-day prison life and the infrastructure that provides the activities and systems that are in place inside the prison for the health, well-being, and safety of the inmates. From the governor to the cleaning worker, from the doctor to the prison orderly, from the chaplain to the kitchen staff, they all contribute to make the prison a vibrant, volatile, or vitriolic working environment. It will also provide valuable information to the students of criminology and sociology in terms of research in reducing recidivism, social inequality, and deviant behaviour and desistance—the final curtain of a criminal career. This is also a book which will, I hope, be invaluable to prison and probation officers in ascertaining what programme really works for transformative reintegration for the recidivists.

The author has a first-class master's degree in physics from the University of Gauhati, a PhD in molecular physics from the University of Leeds, an MEd in science education from the University of London, and a postgraduate certificate in education from the University of Sussex. He taught undergraduate physics students for two years at the University of Khartoum, Sudan, and for another two years at the University of Tripoli in the 1970s. Presently retired, he lives in suburban London with his wife, Puspa. His daughter, Santana, lives in Chippenham near Bath with her husband, Mark, and two sons, Cade and Bailey. His son, Biraj, lives in New York City with his wife, Heather. He is an international opera singer (countertenor).

This book is dedicated to the global prisoner community with sincere hope and prayer that they will see the light at the end of their criminal journey and come to the fold of the normative human society.